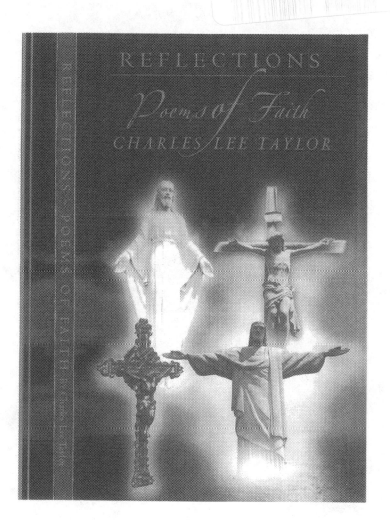

REFLECTIONS
Poems of Faith
CHARLES LEE TAYLOR

REFLECTIONS:

P O E M S   O F   F A I T H

CHARLES LEE TAYLOR

iUniverse, Inc.
New York   Bloomington

iUniverse books may be ordered through booksellers or by contacting:

iUniverse
1663 Liberty Drive
Bloomington, IN 47403
www.iuniverse.com
1-800-Authors (1-800-288-4677)

ISBN: 978-1-4401-7070-6 (pbk)
ISBN: 978-1-4401-7071-3 (ebk)

Printed in the United States of America

iUniverse rev. date: 11/10/2009

About The Cover Photo

This photo is the result of putting five prints together.

The sunset with its reflection of the water was taken years ago by the author when he and his family were taking a cruise. The metal cross was from my mother's house. It had been there for as long as I can remember. It is one of the few things that I have that used to be my mother's. The other cross was in front of "Saint Gabriel's Catholic church which was at the corner of 5th and Tyson streets, 4 blocks from where I lived. They now have a new building and they moved that representation of Christ to the grounds of the new building. The one where JESUS is holding His hands as if He were saying "Come unto ME…" is on the outside of 'The Saint Paul's Evangelical Lutheran Church here is BALTIMORE, MD. It is located on Liberty Road just outside the beltway. The one where Jesus holds His arms out to the sides was taken at the top of a mountain in Brazil. As you look at each of them try to find a meaning for you in each.

As these were put together it seemed to be what I wished for this "Faith" edition. The friend who took the several pictures and put them together at first gave me 4 covers with a different Christ on each. When we could not decide she decided to put them all together. Her name is Alicia Burleson, and I am thankful to have her contribution to this effort. I hope that you think it has been worth it.

GOD BLESS YOU ALL!!!

POSIBLE COVERS FROM WHICH I COULD PICK
FOLLOWS THIS PAGE. BECAUSE I COULD NOT
DECIDE, ALICIA BURLESON, MY BEAUTIFUL AND
HELPFUL FRIEND CONTINUED TO WORK HER
MAGIC AND CAME UP WITH SEVERAL COVER
DESIGNS. BECAUSE I COULD NOT MAKE UP
MY MIND I DO HOPE THAT YOU WILL LIKE THE
CHOSEN COVER. YOU CAN LET ME KNOW HOW
YOU FEEL BY SENDING ME A MESSAGE TO WWW.
CHARLESLEETAYLOR@VERIZON.NET. I THANK
YOU FOR YOUR SUPPORT.
CHARLES LEE TAYLOR, POET

REFLECTIONS

Poems of Faith

by: CHARLES LEE TAYLOR

REFLECTIONS
Poems of Faith
by: CHARLES LEE TAYLOR
REFLECTIONS – POEMS OF FAITH

REFLECTIONS

Poems of Faith

by: CHARLES LEE TAYLOR

REFLECTIONS

Poems of Faith

by: CHARLES LEE TAYLOR

About Those Spotlighted Here-In

In this, my third poetry book, I decided to show some work done by some very special friends I have known some a lot longer than others but they each hold a very special place in my heart.

The one I have known the longest is Joan P. Taylor (we are not related). I met her after I graduated from Morgan State University (then college). I applied for a teaching position and she worked at my assigned school. Because I was given a 6th grade class, and she had one also, that made a wonderful base for a friendship and it is still intact today. Her work presented here is one that I loved so much that I asked right away if I could share it with you. She agreed. ENJOY.

The 2nd friend to be presented to you is a lady who comes to play the piano at the senior center where I go. We all love her and love to hear the music she brings to us. Her name is Hilda T. Kelson. I cannot say too many wonderful things about her or the service she gives to the center members. She has a daughter, Lolita, who also writes. The day I met the daughter she recited an original poem to me and it, too, is included. ENJOY.

I also am presenting another friend's creation. He sent it to me some time ago and because I knew this work was on its way I got permission to share it with you also. His name is Phil Cruz and I thank him and the others for their contributions to this work. And then there is Shani and Brenda Crites, both of who I met while on an outing and book signing with The Black Writers Guild. Both ladies gave me what I present to you now. ENJOY.

I also have included a few "UNKNOWNS" for your pleasure. ENJOY.

Charles Lee Taylor. Poet

An Historic Election

On the first Tuesday in November, 2008
An election took place for which most could not wait,
Our desire was to get rid of President Bush,
To throw him out of office right on his tush.

This one of a kind election made history
A giant step forward for both you and me,
The Black vote this year was a large turn-out,
Though many in the "hood" expressed some doubt.

The Presidency, we all knew, had been stolen before,
Extra care was taken as voters came through the door,
Our voice, through our vote, can have a large effect,
We can not look at it holding our heads erect.

The Dreamer's dream materialized, but it took fortyfive years,
The timing of such helped to remove our fears,
Barrack Obama, not judged by the color of his skin,
But by the content of his character and his true self from with-in.

I never thought this would be something I would see,
Maybe my child or grandchild, but definitely not me,
The election filled us with both hope and pride,
Thanking God for those before who fought, bled and died.

As far as we have come we're still as yet not there,
For things in our homeland are neither equal nor fair,
We hear Barrack's message which most did embrace,
He was very effective in his Presidential race.

As smart as he is he cannot bring change without a fight,
It is a must that each of us continue to do what it right,

Keep the dialogues going in your home and community,
Let's make fewer excuses, but demand accountability,

We may have doubted his message "Yes we can.",
But at the end of the day Obama was our man,
November 4, 2008 will never be forgotten,
Voters cut out a small section that, to the core, was rotten.

To see the dream become real, oh, what a reflection,
This shall forever remain "An Historic Election".

Index

A Dog's Life

I got up to go to work
He went out to play,
He didn't have a worry at all,
I had bills to pay.
I carried health insurance,
He really didn't care,
All of his needs were provided
As he barked or gave me a stare.

I have to eat what I'm given,
He doesn't see it that way,
Put down some food he does not want
It will sit until you take it away.

I want to go out for exercise,
He has a will of his own,
I cannot force him to do my will
So I must leave him at home, alone.

We know which of us must deal with stress
To get done all the things we must do,
There are other points which could be made
But I leave it up to you.

There is one thing that I do believe,
Caused by my wonderful spouse,
The next best thing to being a child of God
Is to be a dog at my house.

By Charles Lee Taylor

A Father

Today we honor throughout the land
The one who took us by the hand,
To teach us things we'd need to know,
Like we would reap just what we sow,
A FATHER.

When problems came he always knew
Just what we should or should not do,
No sacrifice was ever too great,
He'd give you food right off his plate,
A FATHER.

Although his love runs true and deep,
He must take care in order to keep
From sparing the rod and spoiling the child,
Even though parenting may be out of style,
A FATHER.

He gladly worked from sun to sun
And hurried home when his day was done,
Helping with homework, drying a tear,
Solving our problems year after year,
A FATHER.

Now out in the world and on my own
And to our Heavenly Father he has gone,
I hope as he keeps watch over me
Not only a son but he also will see
A FATHER.

A Friend

Some people live an entire life
From its inception 'till its end,
And never know what it is to have
A person they know is a friend.

Someone you don't see in your day to day
Activities but when there is trouble,
If they only know what you're going through
They come to your aid on the double.

To give of yourself, to fill someone's need
Is as far as many people will go,
You unselfishly share whatever you have,
And that is why we all love you so.

To just give my thanks with a word, hug or kiss,
Does not somehow convey how I feel,
The appreciation and the love felt for you
Is deep and wide and it's real.

Because your heart is so full of love
Is the reason you do what you do,
I love you so much and I thank God above
To have given us a friend such as you.

A Lesson Well Learned

A little grain of sand,
Held here in the palm of my hand,
Once a part of great castles on the beach,
Once a repairer of the breach,
Amongst millions within my reach

Was chosen from all the rest,
To help bring about the best…the finest in the land.

This tiny miniscule grain of sand.

One day a grain found itself being led,
To a dark secluded sort of bed,
Swallowed up and tightly shut inside,
The appointed host washed in by the tide.

No escape, no release,
This grain became a most annoying beast.

It scratched and buffeted the pliable thing,
A constant irritation it did bring,
To the rubbery sinewy hidden host,
It became what was dreaded the most.

Each time the grain released its whip,
The host tightened its once frail grip,
Its defense was in its once frail grip,
Its defense was in its awesome essence,
A divinely-given ethereal presence,
That compelled the calcified inner wall,
To surround the grain with a pearly ball.

Frequently, we heard the host utter,
We oftentimes heard it even mutter,
"I cannot fathom in my wildest imagination,
How this union could lead to a glorious destination.
Why, If I had my druthers,
I'd rather be like all the others,
Simple oysters in the sea,
With no special destiny".

Ah, but God had another plan,
By which to bless this barren land,
By which to use this tiny grain,
By which to use the oyster's pain.

A plan to help us heed the call,
To help us stand when we would fall.

You see, the agitating on-going tussle,
Caused the oyster's once fail muscle,
To become obedient and mature,
To rid itself evermore,
Of the turmoil and the pain
Wrought by the assignment of the grain,

The DIVINE assignment of the grain.

Now, the lesson this gives to all the world,
Is found inside each cultured pearl…

That…if we would stand without complaint,
If we'd run the race and never faint,
If we would bear our cross…not seeing loss
If we would tolerate the gritty grain,
And suffer silently the pain.

Fight the good fight of FAITH and WIN!!!
And allow God the eradicate sin,

Then maybe we too can one day unfurl,
The Christ in us to a dying world.

Like the beautiful splendid culture pearl…

Like the magnificent cultured pearl.

By Joan Patterson-Taylor
April, 2000

A Look At Christmas

Christmas comes but once a year
And to me that is just grand,
You do not agree with me you say?
Let me tell you where I stand.

The day is centered around what we get,
Involved with presents and such,
Most people get things they do not want
Because they have so much.

We buy a gift for a relative, friend
Or spouse and it looks so nice,
In the store we may look at the gift,
But we only see the price.

There is a deeper meaning that day
Which most of us seem to forget,
The birthday of God's only Son,
Some don't accept Him yet.

Our Savior had a lowly birth
Though He was a King's King,
His birth brought forth a shining star
And choirs of angels to sing.

He came to teach us love and joy,.
And rules by which to live,
Helping others whenever we can,
Always ready to forgive.

So as we look forward to
The day our Lord was born,

Think of the manger and the cross,
The joy of Easter morn.

We giver our gifts at Chrismas but
God gave us the best gift yet,
Try giving the best gift that you can
With no thought of what you may get.

To get in the spirit of the day
Here's one thing you can do,
Give your gifts to someone in need,
'Twill have an effect on you.

We would all come out far ahead
If we could find a way
To live as Christ would have us live
And make Christmas everyday.

Charles Lee Taylor

A Mother

A mother is one who conceives in love,
She carries her baby with care,
Taking care of herself and the unborn child,
Always conscious of the baby growing there.

She will eat, drink and rest as she should
For she knows as time moves along
That whatever she does can affect the child
And she wants it born healthy and strong.

As the child within develops and grows
Her love for it has begun,
And that love will last a lifetime
For a daughter or a son.

'Then comes the day, the blessed event,
She has no fear of the pain,
Her thoughts are not on the liabilities
But are centered on the gain.

The baby is born and in her arms,
Held gently close to her breast,
Of all the babies born to date
She is sure that this one is the best.

She meets the many demands that it makes
As it goes through the early years,
Though it is not easy she is up to the task,
The blood, the sweat and the tears.

For her, too soon the years rush by,
She wonders where the time has gone,

The child she carried and cared for
Stands before her now, fully grown.

She knows she gave it the best that she could
So her heart is satisfied
Another emotion now stands with her love
As she looks upon it with pride

There are many jobs in the world today
One more important than another,
But the one at the top of her list for years
Has been not a wife, but a mother.

By Charles Lee Taylor

A Thanksgiving Prayer

Dear Lord, this family stops right now
So we may say to you
That we are so very thankful
For the many things you do.

Thanksgiving, a day that is set aside
In order to take a hard look
At the many ways that we have been blessed
Because of the road that we took.

There are friends and family members
All around this house,
We thank you for everyone here
Whether relative, friend or spouse.

We know that we need You every day,
Be with each of us right now,
We see your thoughts toward us are good
As before You we humbly bow.

You gave us family and friends as well,
Now we gather around this table
Not only thanking You for the food it holds
But for these relationships that are stable.

We thank You for giving us Your word
Which is just as true today
As it was in all the years gone by
If we would just get out of the way.

We are covered with blessings everyday
Because we accept Your Son,
Our "Thank You" is not enough, oh God,
Even when the day is done.

Lord, as we now sit down to eat
We thank You for the food again,
And for the loving hands that cooked it.
In Your Precious Name, amen.

Charles Lee Taylor

A Thanksgiving Prayer for my Family

Though we often aren't together,
And our sins are quite aware
We'd like to take this time God,
To thank you for our share
To thank you for the blessings
That are shown on us each day
And to thank you for the miracles
You often send our way
The small miracles of love
And having family and friends
And for knowing you are there
And can forgive us for our sins
Thank you for everything
The big and the small
Thank you for our children
Thank you for it all
Thank you for each day
We can say at least we're living
Let us recognize this
And make everyday Thanksgiving

Copyright: Nov. 6, 1980 composed by: Brenda Crites

A Tribute To My Pastor

MANY YEARS AGO MY PASTOR AND HIS WIFE
WENT ON A VACATION, AND YOU CAN BET
YOUR LIFE
THAT NO ONE THOUGHT THAT BEFORE
THEY GOT BACK
HE WOULD SUCCUMB TO A FATAL HEART
ATTACK

THE CHURCH MEMBERS, BEFORE MANY DAYS
WENT BY,
FORMED A COMMITTEE TO OBTAIN THE
PULPIT SUPPLY,
THEY ALSO INTERVIEWED THOSE WHO
DESIRED THE JOB,
UNTIL THEY FILLED IT WITH OUR NEW
PASTOR, BOB.

FOR HIM TO GET MY VOTE, TWO THINGS I
HAD TO SEE,
HE HAD TO SPEAK WELL AND ALSO BE
YOUNGER THAN ME,
HE SAID HE WANTED TO SEE WHAT GOD
HAD TO SAY,
WHEN OUR OFFER WAS ACCEPTED IT WAS A
HAPPY DAY.

TO LEAD HIS FLOCK, AND WORK FOR UNCLE
SAM TOO
WAS AN AWFUL LOT FOR ANY MAN TO DO,
I BELIEVE THAT HE DID FULFILL EACH JOB
WELL,
GOD BLESSED US, THROUGH HIM, MORE
THAN I CAN TELL.

I THANK GOD FOR HIM ALMOST EVERY DAY
EACH TIME IN THE PULPIT, HE'S GOT
SOMETHING TO SAY,
A WORD FROM GOD FOR A CHILD, MAN OR
WIFE,
WHICH HELPS EACH ONE TO FACE THE
PITFALLS OF LIFE.

THE PASTOR HAS GIVEN US MUCH MORE
THAN WE COULD ASK,
HIS HIGHER EDUCATION THRUST WAS A
GIGANTIC TASK,
TO HONOR MY PASTOR TODAY WITH THE
BEST THAT I CAN DO
IS TO SAY "IF WE HAD TO CHANGE, I'M GLAD
GOD SENT US
YOU."

A Trip To Church

It is Sunday morning once again,
Oh, how I wish I could remain
At home in bed and watch T.V.,
But that can never, never be.

So I get up and I get dressed,
For God my family has blessed,
At church I know that I can seek
The strength to face another week.

I walk right in and start to greet
Some others there, then take my seat,
The organ starts, the building rings
With music as the congregation sings.

Each song has a message all its own,
God never leaves His children alone,
His thorn-crowned head and wounded feet
Reserved our place at the mercy seat.

We sing the songs, then say a prayer,
And then the pastor is standing there
To let us know what God has said
As from the Bible His Word is read.

Then comes the Sermon so we can see
Just how God's Word guides you and me;
I say amen and pat my feet
As from God's Word I gladly eat.

The sermon ends and we sing a song,
We ask all those to come along
And join us as we try to do
Those things which God would have us to.

The service ends and I can say
I am so glad I came today;
I turn to leave and hear my name,
Followed by the words, "I'm so glad you came."

The hymns we sang, hearing the pastor speak
Has fortified me for the coming week;
I pray that I won't get marred in sin,
Before I partake of His Word again.

A Wish And A Promise

Sometimes I wish I had been born
Back in the biblical days,
To meet Matthew, Mark, Luke, and John
And get to know their ways.

To take the march with Moses
On His way to the Promised Land,
Observe the Red Sea as it parts,
By the Burning Bush eagerly stand.

Watch David as he threw a stone
With speed and an aim so true,
Watch the prodigal son as he returned
And began His home life anew.

See Shadrach, Meshach, and Abednego
As they walked around in the fire,
Go with Noah's family on the ark
As the water rose higher and higher.

Of all the settings I could choose
The one I would most enjoy
Is being able to walk with Christ
From the days when He was a boy.

To see Him in the manger
On that great day of His birth,
To look upon that special star
Which spoke to all men here on earth.

To be with Jesus day by day
And listen each time He talked,
I feel I would have been truly blessed,
To have walked where Jesus walked.

Being with Jesus as He slept
On a ship being tossed about,
Seeing Jesus in the temple
When He chased money changers out.

I'd love to stand with Jesus
As He called Lazarus to come out
To hear Him speak and share the meal,
At the Sermon on the Mount.

I'm glad I was not there that day
They nailed Him to the tree,
Oh, what a deep and lasting love
He showed on Calvary.

That love still reaches out today,
He calls to you and me,
If we but put our trust in Him,
He said He would set us free.

He will supply our every need,
Including our daily bread;
There is no doubt within my mind,
For that is what He said.

Adultery

On this subject I have something to say,
You may not see things in the same way,
Really think on each point as it is read,
Never let someone married get into your bed.

Such an act leads to heartache and tears,
Both of which may visit you for many, many years,
You may be destined to spend the holidays of life
Alone as they are with the husband or wife.

Also think this point over through and through,
If they cheat on their mate they'll cheat on you,
The one thing you need, which is trust, will be gone,
You will always wonder when you are left alone.

No matter who, what, when or where
There is no future in it if you have to share,
A lover or mate who goes out with the spouse,
Never out with you but always in your house.

Your emotions took over the relationship you say,
Throw them out, pull it together, start a new day,
It's much better to travel life's road all alone
Than to have a mate that is not your own.

by Charles Lee Taylor

Ain't God Good

AS THE YOUNGEST CHILD OF MY MOTHER
WHO TAUGHT ME AS I GREW UP IN THE
HOOD
THAT NO MATER WHAT LIFE MAY SEND MY
WAY
I CAN ALWAYS SAY "AIN'T GOD GOOD?".

MANY TIMES IN THIS JOURNEY WE CALL LIFE
THINGS DO NOT HAPPEN AS WE THINK THEY
SHOULD,
THE DEVIL MAY HIT YOU WITH HIS VERY
WORST
BUT OUR GOD CHANGED IT TO WORK FOR
OUR GOOD.

I THANK GOD FOR MY FAMILY AND FRIENDS,
I GIVE HIM PRAISE EACH DAY AS I SHOULD,
I LEARNED TO SAY THROUGH PAIN AND
TEARS
THAT THROUGH IT ALL, "AIN'T GOD GOOD?".

HE GAVE US HIS WORD BY WHICH TO LIVE,
WE'VE LET THE ENEMY KNOW JUST WHERE
WE STOOD,
CLAIM ALL OF THE PROMISES IN THE HOLY
BOOK
AND TELL THE WORLD THAT OUR GOD IS
GOOD.

HE GAVE ME A WIFE CREATED JUST FOR ME,
SHE SUPPORTS ME AS ANY WIFE SHOULD,
SHE ALSO GAVE ME SOME WONDERFUL
CHILDREN
WHICH CAUSES ME TO SAY "AIN'T GOD
GOOD?".

HE HAS GIVEN ME MORE THAN THE 3 SCORE
10,
I DON'T HAVE TO RUN TO KNOCK ON
WOOD,
SHOULD HE CALL ME I COULD USE MY LAST
BREATH
TO SAY THAT OUR GOD HAS ALWAYS BEEN
GOOD.

BY CHARLES LEE TAYLOR

All There Is

I had a thought the other day
To live before you die
You must be able to make a break
From each day as it passes you by.

You cannot live in the yesterdays
No matter how hard one prays,
It does not help to constantly long for
What we call "the good ole days".

It is fun and wise to plan ahead,
To earn, invest and borrow,
Much of what happened yesterday
May control what comes tomorrow.

Dreaming of yesterday or tomorrow
Seems unimportant somehow
If we forget to live today,
For all there is, is now.

By Charles Lee Taylor

Answered Prayer

Did you know that God will always
Answer every prayer?
It does not matter if you live
Over here or over there.

Sometimes He will say "yes"
To the request that we carry to Him.
Our prayer may center on us
Or it may all be about them.

God may also say "maybe"
As we call upon His name,
All things are on His time table
And all His children are loved the same.

His answer may be a loud "no"
Which some will not understand,
But He knows what is best for us
For He holds us in His hand.

The answer could be "Wait, my child
For the time is not yet right."
When He knows the time has come for you
Your request, by faith, is made sight.

By Charles Lee Taylor

Anniversary #39

To be married to you for 39 years
Has really enhanced my life,
Because, after GOD, you're my everything,
My lover, my best friend, my wife.

I hope GOD, in His wisdom,
Before calling me to the other shore
Will continue to bless us together
For another 39 more.

I LOVE YOU!!!

Charles L.

Happy Anniversary

At Retirement

Some people go through their working years
With vim, vigor, and fire,
While others seem to come to life
The day that they retire.

Some people think they will be bored,
To get through the day would be rough,
But they find with the passing of day after day
That each one is not long enough.

There are pros and cons at that stage of life,
Each person should look within,
And put things in their proper place
Before retirement begins.

A pro is now you'll have some time,
To do what you've always desired;
Do this, go there, or just sit and relax,
Since working's no longer required.

A con is you now will be leaving friends
You have made through the many years,
Each heart is saddened and yet filled with joy,
Each face showing both smiles and tears.

I wish you God's speed as you now retire,
May each day in it's turn be divine,
What I feel in my heart could only improve
If the retirement were only mine.

Bible

We know that the bible is GOD's holy word
But do we know its true worth?
Some say the name is an acronym meaning
Basic Instructions Before Leaving Earth.
The earth is not our home, you see,
On our journey we're just passing through,
In order to reach our desired goal
We must do what the Word says to do.
A rich, young ruler went to JESUS one day
Asking how he could keep from being lost,
When JESUS told him what he should do
He was not willing to pay the cost.
That young man was asking about his cost
Because he wished to be sure
To reach Heaven which was his final goal,
But couldn't sell his possessions and give the funds to
the poor.
A man in the bible whose name was not given,
A rich man who died and went to Hell,
Saw Lazarus resting in the bosom of Abraham
Cried to his brothers his story they'd tell.
To believe or not to believe the Word,
It is really up to you,
Your final destination for eternity rests in
What you believe, your faith and what you do.
The ones mentioned earlier did not follow
The instructions they were given to do,

You are still here and in your right mind
So don't let that happen to you.
We must give our lives to ALMIGHTY GOD,
The Savior, JESUS, showed us how,
And since tomorrow is not promised
May I suggest that you do it NOW?

Charles Lee Taylor

Blessed

One night when I got into bed
I could neither sleep nor rest,
This was caused by a large and growing pain
In the middle of my chest.

I climbed out of bed and sat in a chair
But the pain would not leave me alone,
So I got up and headed to my car
And drove to the hospital on my own.

They checked me out from head to toe
And even front to back,
They made sure, without a doubt,
I didn't have a heart attack.

There was something the doctors found,
A spot on my left lung,
Since cancer was not even thought about
Their praises are still sung.

I look back over the many years
Of the pain and the fear of that night,
I was really, really blessed back then,
For GOD let me win that fight.

By Charles Lee Taylor

Bumps

A young man in an Oldsmobile,
They said he ran the light
That caused the six car pileup
On 109 that night.

When broken bodies lay about
And blood was everywhere,
The sirens screamed out eulogies
For death was in the air.

A mother trapped inside her car
Was heard above the noise,
Her plaintive plea near split the air,
Oh GOD, please spare my boys.

She fought to loose her pinned hands,
She struggled to get free,
But mangled metal held her fast
In grim captivity.

She was frightened and then she focused
On where the back seat once had been,
But all she saw was broken glass
And two children's seats crushed in.

Her twins were nowhere to be seen,
She did not hear them cry,
And then she prayed they'd been thrown free
Oh GOD, don't let them die.

The firemen came and cut her loose
But when they searched the back

They found therein no little boys
But the seat belts were intact.

They thought the woman had gone mad
And was traveling alone,
But when they turned to question her
They discovered she was gone.

The policemen saw her running wild
And screamed above the noise
In beseeching supplication,
Please help me find my boys.

They're four years old and wear blue shirts,
Their jeans are blue to match,
Once cop spoke up, they're in my car
And they don't have a scratch.

They said their daddy put them there
And gave them each a cone,
Then told them both to wait for MOM
To come and take them home.

I've searched the area high and low
But I cant find their dad,
He must have fled the scene I guess
And that is very bad.

The mother hugged the twins and said,
While wiping at a tear,
He could not flee the scene, you see,
For he's been dead a year.

The cop just looked confused and asked
Now, how can that be true?

The boys said "Mommy, Daddy came
And left a kiss for you.

He told us not to worry
And that you would be alright,
And then he put us in this car
With the pretty, flashing light.

We wanted him to stay with us
Because we miss him so,
But Mommy, he just hugged us tight
And said he had to go.

He said someday we'd understand
And told us not to fuss,
And he said to tell you, Mommy,
He's watching over us.

The mother knew without a doubt
That what they spoke was true,
For she recalled their dad's last words,
"I will watch over you."

The fireman's notes could not explain
The twisted, mangled car,
And how the three of them escaped
Without a single scar.

But on the cops report was scribed
In print so very fine,
An angel walked the beat tonight
On highway 109.

Unknown

Christmas Day

God sent His Son
From Heaven to earth,
Christmas Day was
The day of His birth.

Jesus came down here
Because man was lost in sin,
The Trinity knew
Death was not the end.

Because man was stuck
In a lifestyle full of sin,
After leaving earth St. Peter
Would not let man in.

We must accept Jesus,
He is the only way,
Our debt was so great
Only Jesus could pay.

I thank The Father
For this measure of His love,
I look forward to my mansion
In the heavens up above.

                                    Charles Lee Taylor

Christmas Gifts

THE CHRISTMAS SEASON IS LOTS OF UN
AND IT LASTS FOR SEVERAL DAYS,
NO MATTER THE CHANGES WE GO
THROUGH
WE LOOK FORWARD TO IT IN MANY WAYS.

AS THE TIME DRAWS EVER NEARER,
WE DECIDE JUST WHAT WE SHALL BUY
FOR EACH OF THE ONES WE HOLD SO DEAR,
OH, HOW THOSE DAYS DO FLY.

WITH ALL OF OUR GIFTS NOW FIRMLY IN
HAND
WE NOW HEAD FOR HOME FILLED WITH
GLEE,
AND WHEN THE WRAPPING HAS ALL BEEN
DONE
EACH GIFT IS PLACED UNDER THE TREE.

THE NIGHT BEFORE THE BIG DAY COMES
IT IS HARD TO GO TO SLEEP,
HOW MANY OF OUR GIFTS WILL WE RETURN,
AND WHICH ONES WILL WE KEEP?

SOME GIFT RECEIVED WE WILL NOT USE,
IT IS CAREFULLY STORED ON A SHELF,
THE BEST OF ALL GIFTS YOU CAN GIVE
SOMEONE
IS A SMALL, BUT REAL, PIECE OF YOURSELF.

By Charles Lee Taylor

Christmas
His Birthday

CHRIST, THE SON OF THE LIVING GOD
HEAVEN IS HIS HOME,
RESCUED MAN WHO WAS DOOMED BY SIN,
IT KEPT MAN FROM IN HELL TO ROAM,
SINCE THE BEAUTIFUL DAY OF HIS BIRTH,
THE ROAD MANKIND TRAVELLED TO
CHANGE,
MOST BELIEVE AND TRY TO OBEY HIS WORD
AND MAKE HEAVEN, OUR HOME, WITHIN
RANGE.
SO ACCEPT HIM AS MESSIAH, SAVIOR AND
LORD.

Charles Lee Taylor

Christmas Prayer

I said a Christmas prayer for you
Because the season's near,
I didn't ask for riches
But for gifts so much more clear.

I asked for joyful gatherings
With your family all around,
And for carols to inspire you
With their old familiar sound.

I asked for quiet moments
In your heart on Christmas morn,
For a special time to celebrate
The Savior who was born.

I asked for friends to send their best
That you might know they care,
I asked for peace and love and hope,
And I know God heard my prayer.

Unknown

Christmas Shopping

The time is getting late
And I have so much to buy,
So I can no longer wait
Letting that sleeping dog lie.

My shopping list has now been made,
I must get in the race,
Searching through much stuff to aid
My looking in the right place.

I find that this is not a lot of fun
But I must finish with grace,
Getting desired gifts for everyone,
Yet beating the clock in this race.

It took days, but I got it done
Which caused me to stand and cheer,
Yet we must remember JESUS, The Christ,
Who brought the first Christmas here.

When God gave Christ as His gift to man,
One which could expire never,
It gave mankind a needed lift,
A gift that would last forever.

Charles Lee Taylor

Cleaning House 2006

Last week I threw out worrying,
It was getting old and in the way,
It kept me from being me,
I couldn't do things God's way.

I threw out a book on my past,
Didn't have time to read it anyway,
I replaced it with new goals
And started reading it today.

I threw out hate and bad memories
But remembered how I loved them so,
Got me a new philosophy, too,
Threw out the one from long ago.

Brought it some books which are called
"I Can", "I Will", and "I Must",
Threw out "I Might", "I Think" and "I ought",
You should have seen the dust.

I ran across an old, old friend,
Haven't seen him in quite a while,
I believe His name has always been GOD,
And, yes, I really like His style.

He helped me to do some cleaning,
And added some things Himself,
Like Prayer, Hope and Faith,
Yes, I put them all on a shelf.

I picked up this very special thing
And placed it at the front door,
I found what I call a perfect peace,
Nothing gets me down anymore.

Yes, I've got my house looking real nice,
It looks good all around the place,
For things like Worry and Trouble
There just isn't any space.

It's good to do a little house cleaning,
Get rid of some things on the shelf,
It sure can make things much brighter,
Maybe you should try it yourself.

Author Unknown
Rewritten by Charles Lee Taylor
9-29-06

Demonstrated Love

The Trinity sat talking one day,
Father, Son, and Holy Ghost,
Each felt that He was really the one
Who loved mankind the most.

The Father spoke of when He made
So many things, and all
Were put here for the use of man,
Long before the fall.

Although the Father gave to man
All things he would ever need,
Man still developed sinful traits
Like avarice and greed.

The Son recalled how God hates sin,
And all mankind was lost
Until He left His home on high
To hang upon a cross.

Although His life was sinless
Christ knew He had to die
To prepare the way to eternal life
For mankind if he would but try.

The Holy Ghost began to speak,
He told just why and when
He came to earth to stay with man
Til Christ would come back again.

He knew the hardships man would face
On a road narrow, long, and dim,
A successful trip would be enhanced
If we are comforted by Him.

The one thing which could move them all,
On earth or in heaven above was
The small word representing so much
L-O-V-E, love.

Disciplined Freedom

I heard a preacher speak today,
His words were for you and me,
They centered around the general theme
Of what it means to be free.

When GOD designed and fashioned us
He gave us a free will
To use within a set of boundaries,
And it is that way still.

Adam and Eve were first in line
With things they could not do,
The dos and don'ts have always been
For them, for me, for you.

Some like to think of freedom
Without boundaries of any kind,
One says that just because it is theirs
One can do whatever enters their mind.

Because of this society suffers,
At home we lock ourselves in,
There is danger today whether inside or out
Because some act without discipline.

We fail to guide our children,
Or correct them when they do wrong,
They think they can do whatever they please
As the journey of life moves along.

We have come to a point in the world today
Where to kill is an acceptable thing,
We steal, we lie, we cheat, we scheme
And some done in the name of The King.

There's one thing I'd like you to understand,
Let this hit you squarely on the chin,
Your freedom today and forever more
Must stop where Others' begin.

Charles Lee Taylor

Emotions

We all have emotions telling us what to do,
Think we're in control, no, they tell both me and you,
That's why some love one and some love another,
They control how we feel as we deal with each other.

We all have our own ideas, meek or mild,
As to how we should respond as we raise a child,
We may feel that we failed as a father or mother
If we express more love for one over another.

Just take a look at the bible, the word of GOD,
The directions given there are not that hard
But are there to tell us just what we should do,
And favoritism is shown there in thru and thru.

Pharaoh's choice was Moses, not his own blood son,
And Joseph was without a doubt his father's chosen one,
The prodigal son found himself and he returned home,
Dad was happy but brother wished he'd continue to
roam.

John was the disciple we are told that Jesus did love,
So it must be right if one person is placed above
Even if they are a major part of a whole,
Emotions make the choice, not your mind, body or
soul.

                                        Charles Lee Taylor

Evaluate Self

In order for you to feel good about self
Must you look down at another?
If they seem to do better than you
Does that make a liar of your mother?

Most others must be twice as good
In order to reap the reward
Of income, position, and material things
That you get by not working too hard.

The "Peter Principal" only works
For the ones who are in charge,
But most of us can relate to a plan
Which leads to our living large.

No matter how you feel about me
I wish only the best for you,
My life has been good, though some are unfair
In what they say, think and do.

It is wrong to seek your joy and worth
By looking down on another,
The better way for all concerned
Is to accept everyone as sister or brother.

By Charles Lee Taylor

Falling Snow

As I look out my window
I can see the falling snow,
The only reason that it looks so nice
Is that I have no place to go.

This is the first snow of the season
And winter is not yet here,
I hope that this won't be the norm
Making snow lovers stand up and cheer.

This time I am sick in hospital,
And today I have no desire
To be discharged and journey home
And sit by the fireplace's fire.

The snow may look good while falling
But it holds a trap within,
If you must get out move slowly
So you don't slip and fall on your rear end.

Take care of yourself as best you can
And do what you know you should do,
Never forget in whose hands you rest
For HE will take care of you.

By Charles Lee Taylor

Family

Of all the institutions that
You or I will see,
None can be ranked higher than
The one called family.

Its makeup is so simple,
There are fathers and there are mothers,
There also may be aunts, uncles, cousins
And even sisters and brothers.

Each member has a role to play
No matter where they live,
Each offspring must be taught so much,
Each member ready to give.

When mother was the primary caregiver,
Society as a whole
Was better off for we were not
So callous nor so cold.

Father worked on many levels
To pass his values on,
An honest day's work for one's pay
Was passed down to daughter and son.

The children were taught to love and respect
Someone of a different race,
The saint as well as the sinner
Deserves uninvaded space.

By Charles Lee Taylor

Feelings

I like you, I really do you know,
Because of what you say and what you show,
You've said many times that you're my friend
And you show it to me again and again.

You seem to know when my day is bad,
Or if I'm happy or my heart is sad,
When the problems of life I must pass through
I can always rely and count on you.

You have walked with me in the rain,
Heard me cry out and felt my pain,
Seen me vent and cry tears of joy,
Our love and friendship time cannot destroy.

I don't know just what I would do
Were I to find I could no longer count on you,
You still fulfill a great part of my life
And I love you so much, my Darling, my wife.

Charles Lee Taylor

Forever Yours, Or Am I?

Sometimes I think I'm losing you
Which plays games with my head,
Before I lose you or your love
I'd rather see me dead.

You really mean the world to me,
I've told you that for years,
Expressing my love through words and deeds,
Through smiles as well as tears.

I would not trade the years we've had
For anything at all,
I stand today, as years ago,
To answer when you call.

I beg you not to lose the faith,
I'm yours in every way,
Our yesterdays are memories,
Don't mix them with today.

I made a vow to GOD and you
The day you took my name,
And since that time we have come far,
No two days were the same.

Remember, reflect, or even gloat
Over those things we have done,
Take care a ghost from yesterday
Doesn't give you cause to run.

Hold on to love, to faith and trust,
Those things have gotten us through
The pitfalls we have had in life
Each time they come anew.

I may not know what is on your mind
But you need have no fear,
As long as you desire it, Darl,
I shall remain right here.

By Charles Lee Taylor

Forgiveness

I once worked for a man called "JD"
Who seemed to find joy by picking on me,
The union protected me as best it could,
"JD" could change if only he would.
I asked my God to take him off my back,
With several ministers I tried to make a pact,
The problems continued so I asked God to change
The man or cause me to get out of his range.
One day he came over to me to attack,
I asked once again that he get off my back,
I told him that God said that I should not fear
One who could only destroy my body down here.
Change did not happen until I asked that God
Would bless him and his family, it wasn't hard
To forgive him for all that he had done,
Because he must answer to THE FATHER, THE
HOLY GHOST, AND SON.
"JD" and I have since parted as friends,
Between us there were left no loose ends,
As He did for me, God will also fight for you
If you get in the Word doing what He says to do.

By Charles Lee Taylor

Freedom's Cost

Our ancestors came to this land to be free
And they passed it down to you and me,
Most of us feel that we have the right
To live as we wish both day and night.

We love the freedom which we all enjoy,
But it is not free for we must employ
A large standing army always ready to go
Anyplace on earth as we all know.

They place themselves regularly in harms way'
Which helps keep us safe day after day,
We owe them so much for what they do,
Protecting the homeland along with me and you.

You would know that freedom has a cost
If a member of your family was ever lost
As he or she defended our land
Or the values held as together we stand.

The cost of freedom may be high indeed,
To protect it we must take the lead,
And as I close, I once again say
Freedom is not free, someone must pay.

By Charles Lee Taylor

From Me To You

To Amy Shivers Taylor, the joy of my life,
You're a near perfect woman in your role as my wife,
We've been together for many a year
yet my love has grown and you've become more dear.

When your brother died it was plain to see
That all the boys became your brothers, all but me,
I wanted to become a brother but I would bet my life
You had thought beyond sister all the way to wife.

You know that I never did believe in going steady
But I asked you to marry me before I felt I was ready,
You called your mother and said with a grin
"If you don't mind, Charles, will you say that again?"

We've come a long way, we two, you and me,
And if GOD wills it I hope that will be
Just a sample of what life still holds ahead
And that you'll be mine 'til the day I am dead.

HAPPY ANNIVERSARY

CHARLES L.

Get A Plan

As a youngster goes through life
If they but fail to plan,
Then their thrust is to plan to fail
Whether a woman or a man.

Every trip that we go on
Must have a destination,
In circles if we just run around
The result is only frustration.

But when you have a goal in mind
And map out a strategy,.
You'll find that it is not that hard to do,
To be all that you can be.

Draw inspiration from where you can,
There is plenty of help around
For those who build and work a plan
That is realistic and sound.

GOD placed you in the greatest land
The world has ever known,
HE'S now looking over your shoulder
To see what you do on your own.

Try to decide as soon as you can
Just how and what to do
To reach your goal for happiness,
It's all really up to you.

By Charles Lee Taylor

God Is

Have you ever met the great "I AM?"
Your sins washed clean in the bloom of the Lamb?
Do you know that all of His motives are true
And aimed toward only the best for you?

Have you ever come to the end of your rope
And wherever you looked could see no hope?
Did you hear Him say He'll provide your needs
But you must ask and plant your 'giving' seeds?

Look around and you'll see you can't beat God giving,
Realize that without Him you are not really living,
Free will dictates that He does not hold your hand,
But He will help you to do all you think you can.

His power is infinite, it has no end,
It will work for you if He calls you friend,
You can handle all the trouble, grief and strife
As long as GOD is the center of your life.

Charles Lee Taylor

God Spoke

God spoke to me this morning,
He asked me where I had been,
I was asked if I could tell Him
Why I was still living in sin.

I knew that I had been trained
In the way according to His word,
To hear the truth and ignore it
Was nothing less than absurd.

To say that I was sorry,
God could easily tell
I wished to stay on the road
That took all travellers to Hell.

I asked that God would change me
Into the person He would have me to be,
He answered my prayer and I was saved,
For now and for eternity.

Charles Lee Taylor

God's Call

Early one Sunday morning, GOD, from His heavenly throne
Called the angel of death to Him for an assignment of his own,
Father God mentioned His child, Esther, Who had served Him for many years,
She had endured what life has dished out, the blood, the sweat, the tears.

The angel of death got his assignment and rushed out to his steed,
Making sure that he would take with him the things that he would need,
His assignment was GOD's Esther, though some of us called her "Mom",
He'd be sure that the transition was flawless; no doubt, no pain or harm.

When he got to the destination he found her sitting at rest,
Taking in the beauty of Christmas, the tree and all the rest,
Things of this special time of year which she did love so well,
She did not hear the angel enter suggesting she bid us farewell.

It was not long before she knew her time had come to go home,

To a mansion in a house not made by hands from which she'd never more roam,

She closed her eyes, let her body relax, so the angel could have his way,

As much as we will miss her, she's in a much better place today.

When she got to heaven and stood before that magnificent great white throne,

At no time was she intimidated because she stood there alone,

GOD let her see our sadness, offered her another ten years or more,

She smiles and said "No thank you Father, been there and done that before."

Charles Lee Taylor

God's Love

Just why does God love us?
I really cannot say,
But I know according to His word
He is with us every day.

No matter what things we may do
He is ready to forgive,
His desire is for each of us
To follow His word as we live.

Some may feel it is weakness
To turn the other cheek,
I tell you it requires a lot,
Not for the meager or the meek.

When He said to treat our brother
As we wish to be treated by Him,
What a foundation for life that set
for us as well as for them.

God's plan is still working,
He knows what He wants to do,
His word shall not return to Him void
Whether its object is me or you.

Charles Lee Taylor

Growing In The Valleys

God,
You showed me so many things, like
An answer to prayer can be "No",
We praise Your name because now we see
that it's in the valleys we grow.

My life with Christ has taught me this,
When I have a problem to God I go,
We seek to have a relationship with Him
When it's in the valleys we grow.

God wants to hold us close to Him,
We cannot beat Him giving,
As He gives to us, so many gifts,
He makes us ready for living.

Give God your life, He loves us all,
Stay close to him so you will know
The things in life that will make you strong
Because in every valley we grow.

By Charles Lee Taylor, poet

Happy Day

I never though I'd be alive
To reach birthday number 65,
To me it is supremely clear
That God desires that I be here.

I've done some right, I've done some wrong,
never thinking that I would live so long,
But life's been good I gladly say,
And I feel good on this special day.

To have so many folk wish me well
Brought me more joy than I can tell,
I know that time will become more dear
As I walk through this life year after year.

Life may be as sweet as a honey comb
But should GOD choose to call me home
I tell you now so you will know,
I hope to be ready and eager to go.

By Charles Lee Taylor

He Is

You say you really don't believe in God and
You really don't believe He is real?
All of what you believe must be based
On what you can see, taste or feel.

Children are being kidnapped, or worse, too often,
Women are brutalized and raped every day,
The worst is yet to come it seems,
Yet no "GOD" steps in the way.

You lose your job, your house, your car,
Your life is on a downhill skid,
You throw the blame on "GOD" for all these things
But let me tell you what He did.

He sent His son to earth to save
A world so deeply marred in sin,
He fixed a place for us on high,
He'll take us there when He comes again.

You ask how God lets sin filled men
Do all of the things that they do?
Whether you believe or don't believe,
Know that God believes in you.

Charles Lee Taylor

Heavenly Father

Heavenly Father up above,
Please protect the girl I love,
No matter when or where she may be,
Please keep her safe and unhurt for me.

I love this girl with all my heart,
Life is not the same when we're apart,
I thank you for the day she came
Into my life and took my name.

She is my helper day in and day out,
Our love is kept strong, there is no doubt
Of her position within my life,
She is a near perfect Mom and a wonderful wife.

I ask that You will allow her to live
Many more years so that she may give
To others as she so long has done for me,
Heavenly Father, this is my prayer to Thee.

Charles Lee Taylor

He'll Find A Way

At times the load is heavy
At times the road is long,
When circumstances come your way
And you think you can't go on,
When you feel you're at your weakest,
Jesus, who is always strong,
Will provide for you an answer
When you think all hope is gone.
HE'LL FIND A WAY!!

At times your heart is breaking
With a pain that is so intense
All you hold is broken pieces
To a life that makes no sense.
He wants to lift you up and hold you
And mend each torn event,
He'll pick up all the pieces
That you thought had all been spent.
HE'LL FIND A WAY!!

For I know if He makes the sunset
And put all the stars in place,
I know if He raises up mountains
And the storm tossed waves He can erase,
If He can conquer death forever
To open Heaven's gates,
Then I know, for you, by His Father's right hand
On His throne He doth sit and He waits.
HE'LL FIND A WAY!!

BY: Charles Lee Taylor

His Birthday

Christmas time is here again
When we celebrate the birth
Of Jesus Christ who became flesh
And walked among men here on earth.

Man had gone so far astray
Our lives were filled with sin,
God knew that we would all be lost,
Jesus came and He's coming again.

As we remember the day of His birth
Let us reflect on why He came,
God gave the sinner another chance,
And another in Jesus' name.

He also taught us how to love
Our enemies and to forgive
Those sisters and brothers who do us wrong
As together we try to live.

He said that we should share the things
He put upon the earth,
He said and did so much for all
But had a humble birth.

He showed us just how we should live,
And gave us the rules to go by,
He taught us how to pray for strength
To God who reigns on high.

He promised if we but believe in Him
Our lives will never end,
Trust in His Word, lean on His arm,
He is Savior, Redeemer, and Friend.

It is time we had a Christmas Day
Emphasizing what it is all about,
Keeping it on a higher plane,
Leaving materialism out.

The Wise Men laid their gifts beside
The manger in which He lay,
But He was the greatest gift of all times,
And that gift is still good today.

As you prepare your gifts this year,
Remember the precious fount;
No matter what the gifts may be
It is the thoughts that count.

On the first Christmas many years ago
God gave the world His Son;
At Christmas time and all year through
Give of yourself to someone.

His Chair

I went to see an old friend one day
Who had been sick for quite a while,
I was told he did not know how to pray
And he thought it had gone out of style.

I told him that prayer was alive and well,
Talking to GOD would be easy if he
Would say the things he wished to say
To GOD as if he were talking to me.

He put a chair in which Jesus could sit
Right next to the head of his bed,
He didn't allow any other to use it,
At least this is what he said.

One day his sick and worn body shut down,
When they found him he was already gone,
But one thing that amazed the folk in his town
Was they knew he did not die alone.

His head was resting in the empty chair
With a beautiful smile on his face,
He's gone, we'll miss him but we don't care
For he know now he's in a much better place.

Charles Lee Taylor

His Love

God so loved the world that He gave
His only Begotten Son just to save
The human race so immersed in sin,
Giving man a life that would have no end.

It is His wish that none should be lost,
And he was willing to pay the cost,
He did everything that He had to do
To make a way for both me and you.

Christ said that He was going to prepare
A place for the saved up in the air,
The city called Heaven is really our home,
When we move in there no more shall we roam.

The things done by GOD are and shall be
Based on His love for you and for me,
His thoughts towards us He pronounced them "good",
We give Him praise and glory as we should.

I love The Lord, and I know He loves me,
Just look at me and you will have to see
How many ways He has touched my life
As He used friends, children and wife.

If you let GOD have His way in your life
He may decrease the valleys, trouble and strife,
This paves the way to your heavenly home,
And once you are there you shall never more roam.

Charles Lee Taylor

His Name

When Moses was given the assignment
To go to see the great pharaoh,
God's message to Egypt's leader was
To let His people go.

Moses really did not want the job
But he asked so he would know
Just who it was that was sending him
With such a message for the great Pharaoh.

God did not say "I Was" you see,
For if that were the case
We would still need The Lord to come
To save the whole human race.

He did not say "I Shall Be"
Which would mean He is not as yet,
Therefore we would have no savior
Making Hell in eternity a sure bet.

God said He is the great "I Am",
He was there for all on that day,
His name has always remained the same,
For He has never gone away.

He has not changed from that day to this,
He is the beginning and the end,
He is known by other names, such as
Redeemer, Father, and Friend.

Charles Lee Taylor

Holding Hands

As we walked along holding hands
On a week-end afternoon,
There was joy around everywhere
For a family gathering would take place soon.

A young lady whom we did not know
Came driving down the street,
She had to stop to let us know
Our holding hands, she thought, was neat.

We told her we were man and wife
And had been so for over fifty years,
This made her joy really increase
And her eyes began to fill with tears.

Her deepest desire was to find someone
Who could relate to her that way,
I told her to pray and then let God,
He'll send her His choice one day.

If you are His child God has someone
He has created just for you,
Read His word and live in His will,
He will always see us through.

Charles Lee Taylor

I Believe

Shortly after the beginning
There was Adam and Eve,
And I do believe that God
Meant for man to receive

The institution of marriage
As ordained by God,
If we but follow His rules
It really is not that hard.

To cling to each other
Is not that hard to do,
If we would follow God's own plan
One would be formed from two.

In His word God said
His thoughts toward us are good,
Man cannot improve on this
In the suburbs or in the hood.

God knows best for His children
No matter how we feel,
Whatever comes from the God-head
Is the best and, above all, it's real.

Charles Lee Taylor

"I Didn't Realize"

Woke up this morning not feeling well, negative as
could be,
I didn't realize that the devil was working on me,
I had to have my coffee, and a bun on the side,
I tried not to show it, but my anger I couldn't hide,

On my way to work, I saw this homeless man,
Standing on the corner, with a cup in his hand,
He ask me for a quarter, and I mumbled no,
I didn't realize, this man had no where to go,

I finally got to my desk; it was loaded down,
I thought to myself, I should turn around,
Then the telephone rang, and I grab it real hard,
The voice on the other end said this is God,

I didn't say a word, I wasn't sure of the voice,
The man on the other end said you have a choice,
While you're feeling sorry, you don't understand,
When you woke up this morning, you shook the devils
hand,

He made you mistreat a man, that was in need,
If you would have helped him, it would've been a good deed,
When you got to work, you complained the whole day,
Now that I've got your attention, this is what I have to say,

If you would have prayed, the night before,
You would have been protected when you walked out the door,
But you took for granted that all was well,
You didn't even realized I caught you when you fell,

I'll be with you everywhere you go, but don't assume what's right,

Don't forget that I'm the creator of both day and night,
I already know what you're going to do, before for you do,
Because of my grace and mercy, I still love you,

I love you because you're a child of God, not for who you are,
I have things for you to do that's why I bought you this far,
Now when you wake up this morning, have a smile on your face,

So I won't have to call again, this conversation never took place,

Phil Cruz
05/26/07

I Saw God

When I looked at the many things that you do
To offer a helping hand,
You met the needs where they were found
With an attitude that was grand.
I SAW GOD.

I looked at the sun rising in the sky,
The rain as it fell to the ground,
A large flock of birds as they flew by,
The different seasons as they came around.
I SAW GOD.

I saw what you did for a family in need,
You give help in any way that you can,
As you continue to plant the compassion seed,
The fulfillment of His wonderful plan.
I SAW GOD.

Then came the day you saw His light
And your face was all aglow,
You had walked here many a day and night,
But now to your reward you must go.
I SAW GOD.

Charles Lee Taylor

In The Hospital

When I must go to the hospital
I really don't mind at all,
There are so many good people there
Who answer my beckon call.

No matter what the cause may be,
As far as I can tell
They are dedicated to the goal
Of making me whole and well.

The kindness, concern and professional care
That they have shown to me
Has helped me to get much better fast
As all around could see.

We prayed for GOD to guide them
In what they had to do,
For HE said if you only ask
HE will take care of you.

The ones on staff charged with my care
Must do the things GOD planned,
For HE still holds our all in all
Securely in HIS hand.

By Charles Lee Taylor

IN THE VALLEY

God, You showed me many things,
An answer to prayer can be "no",
We praise Your name because now we see
That it's in the valley we grow.

My life with Christ has taught me this,
When I have a problem to God I go,
We seek to have a relationship with Him
When it's in the valley we grow.

God wants to hold us close to Him,
We cannot beat Him giving,
As He gives us so many gifts
He makes us ready for living.

Give God your life, He loves us all,
Stay close to Him so you will know
The things in life that will make you strong
Because in every valley we grow.

By: Charles Lee Taylor

IT'S BEEN
A
Long, yet wonderful,
Ride.

THANKS!!

It was 50 years ago today
When we stood before God and man to say
The vows that would bind us two for life,
For that day we became man and wife.

I was not there for the long, long haul
But only for the time we were having a ball,
GOD, who is all wise, had another plan,
He guided you in guiding me from boy to man.

Before too long I was sure that HE
Had put you in my life for the good of me,
My life has been wonderful because of you,
Were you not in my life just what would I do?

You are still the most loved one in my life
As we work toward heaven as man and wife,
The love I feel for you still grows and grows,
This is a fact of life that everybody knows.

Charles Lee Taylor

It's For Real

The most wonderful "happening" of my life
Was the day that we became "man and wife",
What you've done for me only heaven knows,
And my love for you still grows and grows.

You have given me joy and a family, too,
But the greatest gift of all, my darling, was you,
It isn't easy to say how much I love you
And how I place no other above you.

I am sure that when I'm old and gray
I'll love you then as I do today,
For as I write upon this page
I know that my love will ripen with age.

And as the days turn into years,
And as we dry each other's tears,
There may be much I do not know
But this I can say where ere I go.

That if my life were to end today,
With my dying breath I could truthfully say
That in all the world if only one thing were true,
My darling, that thing would be "I love you.".

By Charles Lee Taylor

It's Free

I ask you to pause and look around
And you may just agree with me,
Of all of the things we desire the most
The best ones are always free.

The air we breathe, the water we drink,
The sunlight that comes from above,
Those whom we number as our friends
And the persons who give us love.

A sister or brother who is always there,
A mother and a father, too,
All of whom are really priceless
But it is all given to you.

Nothing we do can make us feel
We deserve all the best in our life,
I realize that much of that listed here
Is a gift from GOD through my wife.

Charles Lee Taylor

I've Changed

Today I was given flowers
For the first time in my life,
Which let me know what emotions
I had so long denied my wife.

They made me feel so good inside
And gave me so much joy
That as I went through life's changes
It was almost impossible to destroy.

To give a loved one flowers
May be the best thing you can do
To lift their spirits and lift their day,
And improve how they feel about you.

God gives us plenty of sunshine
And an ample amount of showers,
Which causes all plants on earth to grow
So we can give each other flowers.

Charles Lee Taylor

Let Us Pray

As we bow before Thy throne
There is much we need to say,
But nothing more important than
Lord, teach us how to pray.

We have been blessed by you, Oh God,
In oh, so many ways,
You protect and watch us through our nights,
You guide us through our days.

We have a bed in which to sleep
And we have clothes to wear,
We have been fed each day we've lived
Thanks to Thy loving care.

We have a family filled with love
Many friends, good health and a need
Each day that comes to give Thee praise,
And not show avarice or greed.

We always need to thank you
For all that you have done,
No matter whom we think we are
We know that you're the one.

We thank you, Lord, for sunshine,
We thank you, Lord, for rain,
We thank you for Thy loving care,
We thank you for our pain.

We thank you for the grass, the trees
And all the birds that sing,
We thank thee, Lord, we thank thee, Lord,
Thank Thee for everything.

Stay with us, Lord, protect us, Lord,
As long as we shall live,
We all know how to receive,
Lord, teach us how to give.

We strive to live our lives for Thee,
Forgive us when we sin,
And teach us how to forgive each other
In peace and love, amen.

                                    Charles Lee Taylor

Let's Make Believe

Let's make believe that you're at home
Relaxing as you watch "TV",
Your day at work had gone quite well,
You are as happy as can be.

A shrilling bell cuts through the air
You realize it is the phone,
You know that you must answer it
Since you are there alone.

You pick up the receiver and
You say a firm "Hello",
The caller asks if you're a Christian
And you say "Who wants to know?"

The caller then identifies
Himself as being GOD,
Repeating the name in disbelief
Your head begins to nod.

As you and GOD begin to talk
Your mouth gets dry from fear,
He speaks of all the things you did
Or did not do this year.

Sometimes you did not go to church,
Too often for the wrong reason,
Both of you knew where you were
During the ballgame and fishing season.

Sometimes your body was in the pew
But the preacher you did not hear,

And you had not attended Sunday school
In many and many a year.

He spoke to you of stewardship,
Tears made your vision dim,
For you had never in days gone by
Returned His one tenth to Him

You said that with the bills you had
You could not give Him more,
But what good is a house or car
When you are standing at Hell's door?

God said that if you would put Him first
All things He would provide,
No matter what you face in life
He is always at your side.

He said that you should share yourself
As did His only Son,
For how else can we do His will
Or see that His work is done?

Extend a helping hand each day
To anyone you can,
In order for His plan to work
Man must give aid to man.

The phone call ends, the receiver falls,
You know that GOD had your number,
I know that this was make believe
But I pray you will always remember.

Charles Lee Taylor

Living For Christ

To live for Christ we all must do
Those things He doth command,
No matter when or where we are
He holds us in His hand.

He said we are to help the ones
Whose outlook is bleak or dim,
If we do this to our fellow man
We have done it unto Him.

He said that we should worship Him,
Attend church and be glad you came,
For He is always there, He said
When we gather in His name.

We are to always tell the truth
Whether east, west, north, or south
He finds a liar distasteful enough
To spit the same from His mouth.

He said that we should spread His word
No matter where we go,
This is best done by all our deeds,
Not what we say, but show.

He said we are to seek Him first
No matter what else we do,
If we do so then He will add
All other things unto me and you.

We are to tithe by giving Him
One tenth of all we own,
The blessings we receive must come
From the seeds which we have sown.

To live for Christ is not easy,
He never said it would be,
These things and others must be done
If with Him we spend eternity.

L-O-V-E

I cannot think of any word
That I would place above
The little word that means so much,
L-O-V-E, love.

Because of love God gave His son
Who died for you and me,
Because of love Jesus gave His life
On a cross at Calvary.

Because of love we all sacrifice
For spouse, child or friend,
Because of love we learn to forgive
Each other again and again.

To give of yourself and of your goods,
What a wonderful way to say
That you have love enough to share
With someone else today.

To show the world how much you love
Would in no ways be hard
If at the center of that love
We find that the core is GOD.

Charles Lee Taylor

Love Defined

Love is giving, that is why God gave us Christ
He came down from heaven to ransom the human race,
Love is forgiving, so no matter what you do,
All who ask, God covers them with His grace.

Love is not puffed up but helps to keep control,
When you love, time passes, getting better each day
It warms the body young, but makes you feel good old
God put it in place so there is no better way.

Love Me

So you say you love me,
But how am I to know,
Surely not by what you tell me
But only by what you show.

You may see love as a noun,
Something to have or own,
To say you're in love means nothing,
Such evidence must be shown.

So, what have you done for me lately?
If your love can pass that test
Then I will know just how you feel
And life will take care of the rest.

This concept is universal,
No matter what, where, or who,
You really show that you're in love
Not by what you say but by what you do.

                                    Charles Lee Taylor

Love Is

Love is pain, love is joy,
Love is gentle, love is true,
Love is all things to all people,
But for me, Darling, love is you.

Love is a touch, love is a smile,
Love sees red, love feels blue,
Love is a bridge binding two hearts,
But for me, Darling, love is you.

I cannot imagine life without you,
I can in no way ever doubt you,
You are the real value in my life,
The mother of my children, a loving wife.

May the touch, the smile, the pain, the joy,
The all things to all people, the red, the blue,
Flow between us on a two-way street,
Because for me, Darling, love is you.

Charles Lee Taylor

Make Time For Him

I knelt to pray but not for long,
I had too much to do,
I had to hurry and get to work
For bills would soon be due.

So I knelt and said a hurried prayer,
And jumped up off my knees,
My Christian duty was now done,
My soul could rest at ease.

All day long I had no time
To spread a word of cheer,
No time to speak of Christ to friends
They'd laugh at me I'd fear.

No time, no time, too much to do,
That was my constant cry,
No time to give to souls in need,
But at last, the time to die.

I came, I went before The Lord,
I stood with downcast eyes,
For in His hands God held a book;
It was the book of life.

God looked into His book and said
"Your name I cannot find.
I once was going to write it down…
But never found the time.

Unknown

May I?

With your permission I would like to say
When you accept Christ troubles do not go away,
The prince of darkness works very hard
Trying to get us to turn our backs on God.

As you go through life you'll find this is true,
It may seem that bad things always happen to you,
God's word lets us know if we plant the seed
He will supply us with ALL we need.

Give Him your heart and increase your knowledge,
Study His word as if you were in college,
When the word is hidden deep within your heart
It lets your light shine and sets you apart.

When you get up each day put on the armor of God,
Don't spoil the child by sparing the rod,
Obey the word when you know what God will say,
Life is so much better when it is lived His way.

As Satan continues to mix things up
And God keeps on filling your cup,
Let each of us keep on following His plan,
For no matter where He takes us, He's THE MAN.

By: Charles Lee Taylor

Miracles In My Life

I GOT A PHONE CALL THE OTHER DAY
WITH A GREAT OFFER I COULD NOT USE,
IT BROKE MY HEART TO TURN IT DOWN
BECAUSE I REALLY LOVE TO CRUISE.

BUT VACATION PLANS HAD ALREADY BEEN
MADE
AND IT WAS TIME FOR US TO GO,
WHEN I TOLD THE OTHERS OF THE OFFER
MADE
THEY BEGAN TO RUN TO AND FRO.

WHEN THEY GOT OFF THE PHONE THE
PLANS HAD CHANGED,
A PART OF THEM HAD BEEN THROWN AWAY.
WE NOW WERE GETTING ON THE BIG SHIP
BEFORE IT LEFT ON ITS JOURNEY THAT DAY.

WE GOT TO THE HOME OF THE ONE WHO
CALLED
THREE DAYS BEFORE WE WERE TO SAIL,
WE HAD NO PASSPORTS SO WE CALLED BACK
HOME
TO HAVE THEM SENT TO US "EXPRESS MAIL".

THE TIME HAD COME, THE TIME HAD GONE,
THE PASSPORTS SHOULD HAVE BEEN IN HAND,
A CALL WAS MADE TO THE ONE WHO SENT
THEM,
WE WERE TOLD THEY WERE RETURNING TO
MARYLAND.

THE TIME WAS SHORT, WHAT COULD WE DO?
FOR THE SHIP WOULD SOON BE READY TO GO,
BRO PICKED UP THE PHONE AND WOKE UP
HIS CARRIER
TELLING HER WHAT SHE WOULD NEED TO
KNOW.

WITHOUT THE PASSPORTS WE COULD NOT
BOARD
THE SHIP AND MONIES PAID WOULD BE LOST,
WE ALL ASKED GOD TO INTERCEDE
AND MAKE A GAIN OUT OF A LOSS

MY BABY GIRL WOKE ME EARLY THE NEXT DAY
LETTING ME KNOW THAT SUCCESS WAS AT
HAND,
FOR GOD HAD TOUCHED ALL NECESSARY
ONES
TO BLESS US AS NO ONE ELSE CAN.

WE GAVE THANKS TO GOD AS WE ALWAYS DO,
HE STILL RULES OVER MY LIFE,
WE SEND PRAISES UP, HE SENDS BLESSINGS
DOWN
TO ME, MY CHILDREN AND MY WIFE.

GOD IS ALIVE AND DOING WELL
AND HE LOOKS TO HEAR FROM YOU,
"YOU HAVE NOT BECAUSE YOU ASK NOT", SO
ASK,
AND SEE WHAT HE CAN AND WILL DO.

BY CHARLES LEE TAYLOR – 18-03

Morning Prayer

Early this morning when I woke up
I saw the sun above,
I softly said "Good morning, Lord,
Bless everyone I love."

And right away I thought of you
And said a loving prayer
That He would bless you specially
And keep you free from care.

I thought of all the happiness
A day could hold in store,
I wished it all for you because
No one could love you more.

Unknown

Mother

If we could go back through the years
And relive memories dear,
Our hearts would never fill with tears
For we would have no fear.

She lived a life so sweet and clean,
From day to day a smile,
Her heart was one of sweet serene,
She made our lives worthwhile.

A friendly thought, a pleasant word
Was never out of place,
She ne're was a bit absurd,
Endowed with charm and grace.

And now she sleeps, her day is done,
Her memories linger still,
The mission that she sought and won,
Because it was GOD's will.

Written by the grandchildren –
Mrs. Anna M. Green and
Mrs. Hilda T. Kelson
Written for the children
Dedicated to the late
Mrs. Fannie F. Parker

Mother's Day

May this day you see the sincere love
Others express to you,
The friends, relatives and children, all
Have had much to say and do.

Mothers are seen everywhere
And we know quite a few,
I thank God continually
For giving me to you.

Each of us pay you tribute,
Reaching out to you in love,
Sons, daughters and husbands, too
Do this day certify that of

All the mothers no matter where
North, South, East or West,
You are in the top ten
If not the very best.

Charles Lee Taylor

My Friend

We don't visit each other often,
Nor chat on the phone each day,
Your friendship means much more to me
Than chats or visits could say.

I cherish our friendship dearly
Because it comes from the heart,
So for all of the days that are yet to come,
Our friendship will never depart.

From one friend to another,
When one must go thru strife,
I'm here to give you support and say
It's a part of coping with life.

So hang in there my loving friend,
Things are going to get better,
Our Heavenly Father has a plan,
He is the Master to the letter.

Elaine

My God

My god, how I love you
With heart, body and soul,
I give you heartfelt thanks each day,
You are the one who makes me whole.

I praise you Lord of my life,
Supplier of my every need,
I have your blessings sent my way
Because of my giving seed.

Your words still guide me every day,
You show me what things are right,
It's important that I keep in touch
By praying both morning and night.

When I call upon YOU, You're always there.
There is no better place that I know.
Your Living Word is my guide and shield
As through this world I go.

By Charles Lee Taylor

My Needs

Air to breath, water to drink,
Food to eat, a mind to think,
A roof over head, someplace I can lay,
A talk with My Father every day.

Good friends all of whom add joy to my life,
Siblings, children and a loving wife,
To give back the tenth that belongs to Him
With love and joy, not on a whim.

A steady job to help me provide
For those I love, to feel good inside,
To have pace as I walk in the valley today,
To share His love with others, to always pray.

That which I need and desire the most
Is The Father, Son and Holy Ghost,
To turn away from worldly sin,
To get ready for He's coming again.

Make ready, prepare, so you will know
On the day of judgement where you will go,
We can't live alone, that point I concede,
But if you have Jesus what more do you need?

Charles Lee Taylor

My Oath To You

When you are sad I will dry your tears,
When you are scared I will comfort your fears,
When you are worried I will give you hope,
When you are confused I will help you cope,
When you are lost and can't see the light
I will be your beacon shining ever so bright,
This is my oath, I pledge 'til the end,
To you, the mother of my children,
My wife, my friend.

Author unknown

My Picture

As I look at my perception of judgement day
This is what I see,
God, The Father, is the one in charge,
And The Son is there to represent me.

A call goes out to have brought in
The lamb's book of life,
They had to check my relationship with
My fellow man, children and wife.

There were some things I could not face
And I began to rant and rage,
I looked at Jesus and pleaded "Lord,
Do we have to look at that page?"

Some of the things presented there
Caused me to start chewing my cud,
Jesus touched me and said so softly
"It is covered, my child, by the blood."

I was declared "NOT GUILTY" because
Jesus was my Lord and King,
Seek Him first to Head our lives
And the host of heaven will sing.

Charles Lee Taylor

My Prayer

I send this little prayer to you,
God knows all that you're going through,
Always keep your faith in HIM
Whether things seem bleak, bright or dim.

All things come under His control,
No mater if you are young or old,
GOD knows just why He put you there,
You are still under His divine care.

I ask that God will guide the hand
Which implements His divine plan
And all the thoughts He has of you
Will lead you where He wants them to.

May His love and mercy overflow,
His undeserved grace continue to show
That He wants the best for you body and soul
And very soon He will make you whole.

Charles Lee Taylor
5-11-02

My Sickness

One night when I got into bed
I felt a lot of pain,
I got up and sat in my chair
My composure to regain.

The more I sat, the worse the hurt,
I could not stay at home,
I went out, got in my car
And drove to the hospital alone.

A few days had gone by before
They knew what was wrong with me,
A tumor on my left lung wished
To make me succumb you see.

I ended up loosing half that lung
In the year of our Lord, 1985,
And I know that I am really blessed
By God to still be alive.

For seventeen years I have been cancer free,
Which is not what most people do,
For such a condition as I had
Can take you out in a month or two.

I cannot say why a merciful God
Decided that I should live,
I pray that it is not for what I can get
But much more for what I can give.

I say to you, trust in our God
Who always knows what's best,
Accept His Son, increase your faith,
And He will do the rest.

Charles Lee Taylor

My Sixtyfifth

I never thought I'd be alive
To reach birthday number 65,
To me it is supremely clear
That GOD desires me to be here.

I've done some right, I've done some wrong,
Never thinking I would live so long
But life's been good I gladly say,
And I feel good on this special day.

To have so many folk wish me well
Brought me more joy than I can tell,
I know that time shall become more dear
As I walk through this life year after year.

Life may be as sweet as a honeycomb,
But should GOD choose to call me home
I tell you now so you will know
I hope to be ready, and eager to go.

Charles Lee Taylor

My Testimony

You say you don't believe in GOD
And that is based on what you see?
Give me just a few moments and I'll
Tell you what He's done for me.

He knew the kind of man I'd be
As I traveled through this life,
So He sent me a wonderful woman,
She's my lover, my friend, my wife.

Many years ago deep in my lung
A cancer was growing in me,
But now for over fifteen years
God has kept me cancer free.

He said He would provide my needs
And that He has surely done,
I did not get everything I wanted,
But my needs, he met every one.

He owns all things no matter where,
Oil, silver, diamonds or gold,
He'll give you His all if only you
Return to Him your soul.

Charles Lee Taylor

My Values

Today I say to all who are here
The most valuable things in my life
Are my creator and my three children,
Plus my loving and devoted wife.

Because God knows all, there is no doubt that He
Knew who and what I would need,
He sent someone as my controller
And, at times, to take over the lead.

I do not doubt that God meant what He said,
His ways are not our ways,
Humans are limited by time and space
But God has unlimited days.

Get in His word and follow His plan
And you'll find out just what I mean.
You will learn to believe in things unheard
As well as those things unseen.

God has a mate for most of us,
Don't ever doubt His plan,
Because as long as you're in the will of God
You experience what is best for man.

Charles Lee Taylor

9-11-2001

On 9-11-2001 I could not believe my eyes,
For what I was seeing on the tube was a horrible surprise,
It was the lowest of the low, man's inhumanity to man,
Someone decided to attack us using anything they can.

An airplane, no there were four, used only for to kill,
Our enemy on that day had both the desire and the will,
Their hatred for this land of ours is buried in their core,
The acts they did on that day could not show hatred more.

To kill so many people so long before they should
Have had their lives cut off, and just because they could,
Tells a story all its own which makes you want to cry,
A mother, father, mate, sibling gone, but did not have to
die.

One of the lessons learned that day was driven home to
me,
Of the many freedoms we enjoy, none of them are free,
But as the story line was told before that day was through,
Our leaders decided how to respond and what we had to
do.

I thank the Lord for everyone, who paid for freedom that
day,
Let it be known that there are more who are willing to pay,
Whatever it costs to maintain a free life this side of the
grave,
We shall not give up our way of life just to become a slave.

Before someone else decides to attack us without a good cause,
I beg you to take time to reflect, even with a pregnant pause,
With our resolve we shall prevail and you will be defeated,
We'll hit you hard in many ways so that day won't be repeated.

6-23-02
Charles Lee Taylor

No Time To Say Goodbye

He sat while playing on the steps
As a big car came down the street,
Several shots rang out, he began to fall
And landed at his brother's feet.

They went to church to worship God
And thank Him for blessings sent their way,
During the service Satan boldly walked in
Making this their very last day.

They each worked hard day after day
But neither had a thing they could save,
One day, with little warning they reached their end
Brought to them by a gigantic wave.

There are bad things happening everywhere,
Even the weather patterns are odd,
The best protection that you can get
Is to increase your faith in God.

Our Father in Heaven wants us to have
The best in life every hour,
But there are times when we are reminded
That it is He who has ALL the power.

By: Charles Lee Taylor

Now

Some people love to waste their time
Though they may disagree,
But let me tell you how it looks
Day after day to me.

To get up early in the morn
Before our sleep is done,
Then take five minutes to do
What should require but one.

Then once at work the waiting starts,
For coffee break and lunch,
Nothing is done if it can be
Put off while we talk or munch.

The clock moves oooh sooo slowly,
But its hands do go around,
The day was long and hard it seemed,
But, at last, we are homeward bound.

There are things around the house for you
To attend to day after day,
You think about them an awful lot
But television got in the way.

Another day now draws to a close,
Now think, just what did you do?
Your boss did not get what he paid for
And, at home, you had cheated you.

There is a lesson yet to be learned
If someone can tell us how,
There is no TOMORROW or YESTERDAY,
All any of us have is NOW.

Charles Lee Taylor

Oh, My God

Oh, my God, how I love you,
With heart, body and soul
I give you heartfelt thanks each day,
You are the One who makes me whole.

I praise You for being the Lord of my life,
Supplier of my every need,
Your blessings are sent to me and mine each day
Because of my "giving" seed.

Your words will guide me all of my days,
You show me what things are right,
It is very important that I keep in touch
By praying both morning and night.

When I call upon You, You're always there,
There is no better place I can go,
Your Living Word is my guide and shield
As through this world I go.

By Charles Lee Taylor, poet

Our Anniversary

Today we have been together twenty-five years,
Through times of great joy and times of slight tears,
The love and joy I feel today still grows and springs anew,
For all I am or hope to be is all because of you.

I remember our wedding day, a day filled with joy,
I remember the days of our children's birth, two girls and
then a boy,
I remember the day you took a job, in fact you wanted two,
I remember trips and other things, all of which I owe to you.

The love I had on our wedding day has grown a lot since
then,
Most days I even like you, my wife, my lover, my friend,
We both have changed an awful lot since we first said, "I
do",
I hope it was for the better, I know I'm pleased with you.

Of all the gifts that come from God, His many
blessings, too,
The greatest one from where I sit, my darling, is you,
These twenty-five years have come and gone, I hope that
we shall never
Get off this road that leads us to togetherness forever.

*We've shared the ups, - we've shared the downs, and it's been
loads of fun,
I say to you before God and man, "We've only just begun",
Today, my dear, there is no doubt, I'm glad that I'm alive,
I raise my glass looking forward to another twenty-five.*

Our Charge

As we go through this life
We are to do what we can
To serve our God, The Father,
And to help our fellow man.

There was a time
When God went door to door,
But in today's market
He does not do that anymore.

You and I are to always
Help our fellow man,
God could choose another way,
He has the power, we know He can.

If you and I both help
Those we find in need
God will surely bless us
For having planted that seed.

To give of our very best
As we deal one with another,
God will send blessings down
For the child, father or mother.

Charles Lee Taylor

Peppie

Many, many years ago, shortly after I was wed,
A long time before the first child came,
We decided to get a puppy
And Peppie Taylor was her name.

A better dog I could not desire,
She showered us with unconditional love,
But she did not stay with us very long
Before returning to our Father above.

My heart was broken as I watched her die,
Friends told me it was a part of the plan
That God had, to get me to focus on the child
He was sending to help make me a man.

Because the pet was raised on our bed,
Which may have been contrary to style,
She may not give in to the changes required
When God delivered to us a child.

I still miss her now, some forty odd years,
But the daughter who came when she died
Is a wonderful blessing, but Peppie knows
That with God's help its alright, though we cried.

Charles Lee Taylor

Plans Change

WHEN THE WEEK BEGAN WE WERE AS HAPPY
AS COULD BE
BECAUSE BEFORE IT WAS TO END THERE'D BE
A PARTY,
A FRIEND I HAD KNOWN ALL MY LIFE
WOULD CELEBRATE 90 YEARS,
WE LOOKED FORWARD TO THE TRIP AND
ADDING OUR VOICES TO THE CHEERS

TO HAVE A LIFE TO LAST SO LONG SPOKE
VOLUMES ABOUT HER LIFE,
SHE SUCCESSFULLY FILLED SEVERAL ROLES,
LIKE MOTHER, FRIEND, WIFE
HER COOKING WAS OUTSTANDING, THAT'S
SOMETHING I REALLY KNOW,
BECAUSE WHEN IN MY HOMETOWN HER
HOUSE WAS THE PLACE TO GO.

WE STILL ARE GOING ON THE TRIP
ALTHOUGH THE PLANS HAVE CHANGED
NO PARTY NOW WOULD WE ATTEND,
SOMETHING ELSE HAS BEEN ARRANGED,
INSTEAD OF VOICES FULL OF CHEERS WITH
BROKEN HEARTS WE CRIED,
THE GREAT I AM HAD CALLED HER HOME,
OUR DEAR AUNT SISTER HAD DIED.

WE GIVE THANKS SHE WAS HERE SO LONG,
FOUR SCORE YEARS AND TEN,
I KNOW THAT IF GIVEN A CHOICE SHE
WOULDN'T RETURN AGAIN,

THE SEEDS SHE SOWED, THE ONES SHE
HELPED WILL BE REMEMBERED FOR YEARS,
IF WE LISTEN WE MAY HEAR HER SAY "LET
YOUR SMILES SHINE THROUGH THE TEARS"

CHARLES LEE TAYLOR
8-27-02

Reflections

While lying in my hospital bed
Thinking of days working in public schools,
I had quit not because of students but
Those parents who would not follow the rules.

Let me say one thing right here and now
That you should have heard before,
Your beautiful baby, your wonderful child,
Is no better than the one next door.

From the day the child is born
You have a big job to do,
For most of the things done in its life
Will come from its learning from you.

The value of an education,
The results of both hate and love,
The values taught by Jesus Christ
After He left His home above.

They may start out as a part of the curse,
"You will bear children in pain"
But if you see that they are trained well
They will bless you again and again.

Charles Lee Taylor

SAINTS and SINNERS

When somebody yields to temptation
And breaks one of man's or GOD's laws,
We look for no-good in his make-up,
But oh, how we look for the flaws.

No one cares about how he was tempted,
Nor praises the battles he's fought,
His name becomes food for the jackals-
For us who have never been caught.

"He has sinned!" we shout from the house-tops,
We forgot the good deeds he has done,
We focus on that one lost battle
And forgot all the times he has won.

"Come, gaze at the sinner!" we thunder,
"And by his example be taught
That his footsteps lead to destruction!"
Cry we who have never been caught.

I am a sinner, O LORD, and I know it,
I'm weak, I blunder, I fail,
I'm tossed on life's stormy ocean
Like ships embroiled in a gale.

I'm willing to trust in THY mercy,
To keep the commandments Thou'st taught,
But deliver me, LORD, from the judgement
Of those who have never been caught.

Unknown

SALVATION

Have you ever met the great "I AM",
Your body and soul washed in the blood of the Lamb,
The sins of your past were thrown away
As you learned many things like how to pray.

He is always true to His revealed word
No matter if it's read or only heard,
Sometimes influenced by what you do,
But He has things set aside just for you.

He may own everything that we see,
And yet the requirement for you and me
Is to give Him a tenth of all we earn,
A difficult lesson for man to learn.

But if we would follow His divine plan,
Overflow blessings would be sent down to man,
You can let Him lead if you only believe,
He will send you more blessings than you can receive.

Please listen to me and let God have His way,
That is the most important thing I can say,
Our future does not have to be bleak or dim
If we are willing to turn it over to Him.

Charles Lee Taylor
5-4-02

Second Place

I've had these friends for many years
And I know how much they care
About all the things I face in life
No matter what, when or where.

Sometimes we may not talk for weeks
But there is no doubt in my mind
That anytime a real need pops up
They are never hard to find.

It is a fact at this point in time
They have never failed me yet,
I also try to be there for them,
Trying to give at least as good as I get.

Friendship, the second best gift given,
Ordained by God above,
The only thing that is more desired
Is that freely given gift of love.

Charles Lee Taylor

She's Mine

I woke up this morning
Sometime around three,
Thanking God that I have a wife
Who looks out for me.

She blessed me with children
At least two out of three,
And after all these years
She still looks out for me.

One thing we do regularly,
As often as can be,
We hit the road together
For a week or two or three.

And when the trip is over
We're as happy as can be
Because I look out for her
Who continues to look out for me.

If happiness is your goal, my friend,
As from the pitfalls of life you flee,
Let her know that you have her back
And she'll look out for thee.

Charles Lee Taylor

Sin Power

God made Adam a physically perfect man,
He should still be alive today,
The only reason that he had to die
Was that something, sin, got in the way.

When Eve was made as Adam's mate
She, too, was to be around
For years upon years in the garden,
Because her body was also sound.

Eden was such a beautiful place,
It was prepared just for them,
God only asked that they obey
The rules as set down by HIM.

When sin came in, all things changed,
And Adam blamed God for this,
The woman he had been given
Did not heed the serpent's hiss.

Adam now had to till the soil,
He now had to prove his worth,
Eve did not go free for GOD said that she
Must now endure the pains of childbirth.

We need to call upon and lean on GOD
More now than ever before,
HIS love and gifts are unending
And HIS promises I claim more and more.

Charles Lee Taylor

Sometimes I Dream

When I think of how I love you
With every fiber in me, I seem
To make a fictional journey,
Therefore, sometimes I dream.

Because a measure of all my love
Can be seen by the things I give
To you, my love, each day of my life
Which can only be done if we live.

Because tomorrow is not ours,
All we have is our today,
If I know there is something you want
I try to get it for you right away.

Why wait for another birthday to come
Or an anniversary or such,
If the funds are there you get it now
Which is saying "I love you so much."

There is nothing I have you cannot get,
My whole life is under your control,
As are all the things I feel I own
Be it property, silver or gold.

Always remember my love for you
As together we float down life's stream,
At times the funds may not be in place
So that's why sometimes I dream.

Charles Lee Taylor

Speak Of Love

I heard a young man speak of love,
His words rang true to me,
I share his thoughts with you today
For we two did agree.

Love is a strong emotion,
It can make you cry or sing,
The object may be a person,
Or it may be a place or thing.

To really love another
Means that you will more or less
Do those things within your power
To assure their happiness.

Love is not selfish in any way,
It does not seek reward,
You put yourself in second place
Which can be very hard.

You find your greatest pleasures
Come from all the things you do
For and with the one you love,
Even if they don't love you.

The giving which true love requires
Can be a bitter cup,
It shines as bright as any star
When we must give someone up.

No matter what you may possess
Or the style in which you live,
You cannot experience the emotion of love
Unless you are willing to give.

Because someone may give to us
We say we love them too,
But measure your love by what you give
Instead of what is given to you.

Charles Lee Taylor

Speak Of The Dead

All my life I have heard it said
That we don't speak ill of the dead,
We can not tell you just what to do,
But whatever you choose, keep it true.

If John did not live a beautiful life
Where he put nothing in front of children and wife,
When you speak of him, if your words are true,
The hearers can't lay any blame on you.

Our conversation is more than our talk,
It also includes what we do, how we walk,
As we look back at the end of the day
Who is moved the most by what we do or say?

Should I live badly thinking only of me,
Trying to hide my flaws so you cannot see
My methods or motives doing things my way,
Fixing it so that you, not I, should pay.

Try to live with others in peace and you can,
And it doesn't matter if you're a woman or man,
When you meet THE MASTER let the words be true
That your friends and others say about you.

Charles Lee Taylor

Special Blessings

Friends are very special blessings
Given to us by God,
Some folk never have many,
They wish not to work that hard.

To have a friend is not easy,
And it does depend on you,
Friendship is the product of many things
Like what we think, say and do.

You may measure life by friendships,
Whether you fail or succeed,
A better rod to use is where
Are they when you are in need?

I look around and you are here,
You are never hard to find,
God blessed you and you share it,
You are each one of a kind.

You came to help us celebrate,
For that we thank you all,
May God continue to bless you
And hear your every call.

May The Father, who does not change,
Keep us forever in His will,
And as we deal with our daily life
May the friendships remain with us still.

Charles Lee Taylor

Survival

The world is such a crummy place,
That's one thing most folks know.
Why do we then remain on earth?
There's no place else to go.

We must have air and food and drink
If we are to stay alive,
And we can find no other place
Where humans can survive.

God made a good and wonderful earth
Without fanfare or fuss,
And things that have gone wrong since then,
Are all because of us.

Some folk will bring a child into the world
And put it on a shelf,
Expecting it, when the time is right,
To climb down and raise itself.

We all must breathe in poison now,
Because some folk don't care
About the many pollutants that
Contaminate our air.

Our waterways no longer
Do the job they used to do,
We are turning them into death traps,
Killing sealife and mankind, too.

Teach Me To Pray

Please, teach me, LORD, I want to know
Exactly how to pray,
I need some words. Which ones are right?
Please tell me what to say.

I've bowed my head, I have knelt down
But should I be upright?
I've closed my eyes, I've raised my hands,
Or should I fold them tight?

Do I stand up? Should I sit down?
Dear Lord, what do You like?
Are lights turned on or are they off?
Would You like candle light?

Wear my glasses? Take them off?
Be at my desk or table?
Should I whisper? Speak out loud?
Do I quote the Bible?

What do YOU think about the time?
Do YOU prefer the dawn?
Should I pray fast or keep it slow?
Is it better short or long?

I'm new at this, what are the rules?
I want to do it right.
How do I know YOU'LL ever hear
Or that I'm in YOUR sight?

And while I sat there quietly,
Waiting for some sign,
I hear a gentle voice say
"Oh, dearest child of mine…

Do you think I really care
About the time of day?
Or whether you are standing up
Or kneeling when you pray?"

"I don't care about your posture
Or about the place you choose,
Just open up your soul to me,
I have no other rules."

Tell Me what is in your heart'
And tell Me what you seek,
Tell Me of your sorrows
And of the things that made you weak."

"Speak to ME in private
About what concerns you most,
I know about your good deeds…
You have no need to boast."

"My child, you don't need lessons,
Just talk to ME each day,
Tell ME anything you want, dear child,
Anyone can pray."

Unknown

Thank You God

Have YOU thanked God for the blessings
He sent your way today?
Do you ever consider how your life
Could have gone another way?

Sometimes we can't see the forest
Because there are so many trees,
The master may use so many things
To bring us to our knees.

Do you see your life to always be
One operating in the red?
Stop zeroing in on the negatives and
Count your many blessings instead.

Our Heavenly Father knows your needs
And He knows just what to do,
For if He takes you to a problem
He'll surely see you through.

So, don't forget to thank Him
For all the things He's done,
You're always on the mind and in the heart
Of The Father, Holy Ghost and Son.

Charles Lee Taylor

The Beginning

Have you ever been with a loved one
When they came to the end of this life?
If they had gotten ready for the journey
They embarked on it without strife.

When Jesus came to redeem mankind
He said He made death our friend,
By accepting Him, the sole Son of God,
We inherit a life without end.

So when it is time to leave this world
We can do so with a big smile,
At that time we know we'll be with Him
In just a little while.

We shall go through the gates of heaven
And be met by those to welcome us there,
Soon after we find we are worshiping God
From the mansion He built for us in the air.

If you have not made your decision for Christ
Don't put it off further, my friend,
That alone is the only guarantee
To have a life that you will love, without end.

Charles Lee Taylor

The Big War

A certain man had a vision one day,
The outlook of mankind was dim,
He went to a cave deep within the earth
And built a room just for him.

His mainstay would be a computer
That would supply his heart's desire,
He perfected the game of "VIRTUAL REALITY"
As tension between men grew higher.

One day someone pushed the big button,
And someone else did respond,
Missiles were flying everywhere
And the last big war was on.

With everyone on earth annihilated
His room was ready to go.
He felt he was the last man on earth
But, in fact, he did not know.

His program had a "VR" Lieutenant,
She knew even more than did he,
And when he presented the emotion of love
Her mind was thrown slightly off key.

He tried to get her to see things his way,
You only have emotions if you're real,
And since she came from the "VR" world
Even she knew that she couldn't feel.

Her reality was now being denied to her
So she formed an elaborate plan
To insure that hers were the orders obeyed
Instead of those of the man.

When he woke up soon after the break
He could hear a party going on.
After dressing he went out to join the group
He was ignored as though he were gone.

He could not believe what was taking place,
He fell to his knees crying "Lord,
Before we put more faith in others
We should put more faith in God."

Charles Lee Taylor

The Gift

Why do I love Christmas so?
Oh, yes, I have my reason,
The joy and love so prevailing
And other intangibles of the season.

We buy many gifts for relatives and friends
To show them that we care,
Some say that it is not the gift that counts
But the thoughts and intentions we air.

But no gift given or received
By a child, woman or man
Can compare to the greatest gift of all
Which came out of THE MASTER'S plan.

GOD gave His Son to redeem mankind
Who had fallen so deep in sin,
HE saved us once, HIS job was finished,
And yes, HE will come back again.

Charles Lee Taylor

The Day Before Christmas

'Twas the day before Christmas
And I was upset,
I had not completed
My shopping as yet.

I thought to myself
How the time did fly,
But I did still have
Several gifts to go buy.

There's a very long list
With the names "dos and don'ts",
Never buy the undesired
But deal with what one wants.

Follow God's lead,
He gave us His best,
If we do as did He
Then He'll take care of the rest.

There is one more thing
I would ask that you do,
Never give a gift you would not
Want given to you.

Charles Lee Taylor

The Dialogue

I'm falling apart at the seams it seems.

My soul screams.

"Rest." GOD says. "My Child, be still."
I say, "Well who will make sure everything is
accomplished." God says, "I will.

My Child you are weak and tiny, you see.

You often try to fight battles that are meant for me.

You need to learn to let go and let me be the Almighty
GOD I AM."

"But Father," I humbly reply, "I'm just trying to do the
best that I can."

"See that is the problem. You think that this is all about you.

Have you forgotten it is Jesus who sees you through?"

"Father, I am sorry." Tears come to my eyes, I wipe
them aside.

"I know that I am guilty sometimes of having too much
pride.

Please forgive me in Jesus' name." I bow my head down low.

HE says, "You are forgiven. It is My WORD and it is so.

The enemy will try to make you feel ashamed and unworthy.

But remember, my beloved child, you are mine and dear to me.

You will fall short; you will stumble, but repent and try again.
Jesus' blood has already cleansed you of all your sins."
"LORD, you are so wonderful and just. Thank you for your mercy!"
He holds me in his hands and continues to bless me.

Shani

The Fall

One day when God himself had a need,
He drew up a beautiful plan,
Reached down, and from a handful of clay
Designed and breathed life into man.

God provided for and watched over man,
Yet one day He had to believe
That His creation suffered from a void,
So, to fill it, He created Eve.

They were given one basic rule
That they would have to live by,
The Creator told them that without a doubt,
If they broke it, they'd surely die.

Before too long they broke the rule
And man had fallen from grace,
Each realized they had no clothes on,
Shame caused each one to hide their face.

Eve blamed the serpent for what she did,
But Adam gave all blame to God,
From that day, Eve would bear children in pain
While Adam must now till the sod.

Man has lived under that curse since then
But God still shows us His love,
If we will accept His Son and His grace,
We'll join Him for an eternity above.

Charles Lee Taylor

The Gift

Christmas is coming and I know why,
It's because Jesus left His home on high
To rescue man who had sunk deep in sin,
But before He left earth He said He'll come again.

Because man disobeyed God we fell into sin,
Even though we have His word we break it again and
again,
At times we don't know where to go or what we ought
to do,
Our shallow faith will also doubt that He will see us
through.

In order for man to be justified
Some blood would have to be shed,
The only blood which could do just that
Must come from the GODHEAD.

Jesus said that He would come to earth
So that He, mankind could save,
He knew just how much the Father loved us,
He loved us so much that He gave.

So as we get ready to celebrate
The birth of a Savior who knew
That it is more blessed for us to give,
Concentrate on gifts given by you.

                                        Charles Lee Taylor

The King

Every day with Jesus is sweeter than the day before,
No matter how much you love Him He always loves
you more,
And when you get to glory He'll be waiting for you at
the door,
Every day with Jesus is sweeter than they day before.

You cannot beat God giving, all blessings come from
above,
Jesus gave His life to save mankind, what a measure of
His love,
He teaches us to be gentle, not like the hawk but the
dove,
Let it be known where ever you go that you're a child of
THE KING.

By: Charles Lee Taylor
5-19-02

The Last Trip

One day when the telephone rang
I felt it was bad news somehow,
When I answered it I heard my sister say
"I need you. Can you come now?"

Clothes were packed and put in the car
As we prepared for the trip,
While underway a tear would fall
Or I might bite my lip.

My mother had finished her earthly race
And gone back home to God,
To continue my race without seeing her face
Would make the rest of my life a little hard.

I found that I could reach within
And locate the strength I would need,
Most of it had developed and grown
Because Mother had planted the seed.

God really blessed me through her,
She will be with me all my life,
Not only do I thank Him for giving me to her
But for giving me a loving, caring wife.

By: Charles Lee Taylor

The Life I've Lived

Who do you see, people, who do you see?
A crabby old lady who just looks like me,
Look closer, look nearer, I'll tell you who you see,
I am a girl of twenty, sassy, single and free,

In love at thirty and a bride to be,
Things are looking good for my man and me,
At forty I'm mellow, traveling a lot,
Spain, Canada, Alaska's my spot.

At fifty I'm wise, life has taught me so much,
And feeling good about the lives I've touched.
At sixty, retired but I don't slow down,
I read, I sew, I shop all over town.

Quite sad now, I'm seventy, my beloved has departed,
We shared our lives together, now I'm broken hearted,
At eighty I'm mobile, not as mobile as before,
My mind tells my body things I just can't do anymore.

At ninety I'm content, satisfied you see,
My friends, my family look closer to see me,
I'm not a crabby old lady void of a golden heart,
I'm tired and I am lonely and ready to depart.

I'm prepared to meet My Maker, to see Him face to face,
You'll see I'll never die, I'll transition to my heavenly place.
Wipe your eyes, dry your tears, it was time for me to go,
I'll always love each of you, how much you'll never know.

Don't look for me in this body for I'm no longer there,
I've been lifted up to Jesus, now I'm in His care,
If you choose to grieve for me make it short and sweet,
And know that where I am today no power on earth can beat.

By Lolita A. Kelson

Dedicated to my precious Great Aunt
and special God-mother, Ethel, "Joe", Friend
Date entered eternal life – October 9th, 2005.
Forever in our hearts and minds Little Joe.

The Living Word

My dear friend, have you not heard
That in the beginning was The Word,
And although some may consider it odd,
The Word was alive and dwelt with God.

As a real part of the three-in one
The Word knew that something had to be done,
Man had become deeply marred in sin,
His relationship with God to restore again.

God gave The Word a form, new and fresh,
And sent it to earth in the form of flesh,
His job was simply to show us how to live,
Moving closer to God who, if asked, would forgive.

The Word had to pay an enormous fee
For the right of redemption for you and me,
For us He suffered, bled and died,
But is now sitting at His Father's right side.

The Word came and did what He had to do,
What happens now depends on me and you,
He laid out a perfect redemptive plan,
What happens now is really up to man.

Charles Lee Taylor

The Lost

All of my life I have heard folk say
That they found Jesus on a special day,
Their life has not been the same for when
Jesus came in He started casting out sin.

To give your life to Jesus is very good,
He wishes all would do so, and they could,
But we desire to do things our way
Rather than yield to God day after day.

Getting around the pitfalls of life,
Giving us joy to replace the strife,
The word of God has a lot to say,
Use it as a guide, it will show you the way.

What a price Christ paid hanging on that tree
To ransom mankind, and that's you and me,
Jesus was willing to pay the cost,
For He knew it was us, not Him, who was lost.

Charles Lee Taylor

The Madison Queens Say Welcome

I come before you at this time
To welcome you one and all,
Thank you for helping us celebrate
Thirty three years of answering God's call.

We have extended a welcome throughout the years
Which brought us very much pleasure,
To have you with us at this time
Brings us joy almost beyond measure.

Sit back, relax and enjoy this time
Together as we spend it,
God will send the blessings down,
The praise goes up as we send it.

I say thanks again to one and all
By stopping by here today,
Your welcome extends to all levels
Seen in what we do and say.

By Charles Lee Taylor

The Plan

There is a land, so I am told,
Where no one there shall ever grow old,
A land that never has a night
Because it is radiant with The Creator's light.

All of the streets are paved with gold,
When approaching the throne do so as bold
As any other one who is there
Because all there-in are under His care.

There is a supply of milk and honey,
Each day is bright but none are sunny,
You find the place not made by hand
But just for you in this promised land.

As you go through this life, please prepare
To move to your mansion in the air,
Should you run but not win this race
You will end up in another place.

It is His desire that none should be lost,
But some of us will not deal with the cost
By doing those things we are required to do,
Believe it or not, it's really up to you.

Charles Lee Taylor

The New School
PRAYER

Now I sit me down to school
Where praying is against the rule
For this great nation under GOD
Finds mention of Him very hard.

If scriptures now the class recites,
It violates the Bill of Rights.
And anytime my head I bow
Becomes a federal matter now.

Our colors can be purple, orange, or green,
That's no offence; it's a freedom scene.
The law is specific, the law is precise.
Prayers spoken aloud are a serious vice.

For praying in a public hall
Might offend someone with no faith at all,
In silence alone we must meditate,
GOD'S NAME is prohibited by the state.

We're allowed to cuss and dress like freaks,
And pierce our noses, tongues and cheeks,
They've outlawed guns, but FIRST the BIBLE.
To quote the GOOD BOOK makes me liable.

We can elect a pregnant Senior Queen,
And an "unwed daddy" our Senior King,
It's "inappropriate" to teach right from wrong,
We're taught that such "judgments" do not belong

We can get our condoms and birth controls,
Study witchcraft, vampires and totem poles
But the Ten Commandments are not allowed,
No word of GOD must reach this crowd.

Its scary here I must confess,
When chaos reigns and schools a mess,
So, Lord, this silent plea I make,
Should I be shot, my soul please take.
AMEN.

Author Unknown

The Seeds

I tell you this but you may not believe
But God knows it is true,
I have given my last dollar to someone in need
But something always comes to me, too.

I have found that you can't beat God giving,
He has many things planned to give you,
The thing that controls whether they come or not
Is controlled entirely by you.

To hold on to the little we have
With a fist that is clinched so tightly
May cause your prayers not to be heard
As we send them up nightly.

That tight fist says you will not share
As was in The Master's Plan,
It also keeps Him from putting more in
Because of the position of the hand.

God put in His book these very words,
"To whom much is given much is required",
So my sister, my brother, try to get it right
Before your time here has expired.

Charles Lee Taylor

The Sermon

There once was a man named John Henry,
Born and raised in a small southern town,
Wherever he went adults had his mom's consent
To give him instructions which were good and sound?

The day that he finished high school
He was heard to say at graduation
That he would go to college to increase his knowledge
So that he could stay ahead of inflation.

He started to attend college in the fall,
In a town with seven colleges there,
Many students in school followed the rule
And joined a church under its "watch care".

Just as the pastor got up on his feet
John Henry came through the door,
He walked slowly while looking for a seat
And finding none, he sat on the floor.

Deacon Campbell, a young man of 92,
With his walker made his way down the aisle,
When he reached the young man he took his hand,
He, too, sat on the floor with style.

The pastor spoke of what they had seen,
His words they would soon forget,
But the sermon they saw was like a blow to the jaw,
And most remember it well, even yet.

Learning comes from what we hear and see,
Someone may be taking their lead from you,
So wherever you go you should always know
Your loudest message is not what you say but what you
do.

Charles Lee Taylor

The Village

It is said that it takes a village
In order to raise a child,
In that I am a believer
For I was growing up wild.

No matter where I found myself
Someone there knew me,
If I did not act just as I should
Another's eyes would let my mother see.

When I would get back home
Mother would tell me what was said,
I learned better than to disagree
For I could end up dead.

I know that if a loving parent
Does not correct and guide,
When and if adulthood is reached
It could be a real rough ride.

When a parent works at that job
The offspring will be made mad,
When out on their own a change takes place
For now, they give thanks and are glad.

Charles Lee Taylor

The Vow

Were you listening the day you were wed
As the official read the vow?
Those words were true that precious day
And no change from then to now.

On that day you were wrapped in love,
All present could easily see
How full of joy the two of you were
On this day which had to be.

You each promised GOD and each other
That you would do several things,
And should you keep them your marriage would be
Without end, just like your rings.

Every day will not be easy,
But you can make it if you try,
An important thing for you both to do
Is to make "we" more important than "I".

Charles Lee Taylor

The Wedding

I went to a wedding the other day and
As soon as I stepped in the room
The usher looked at me and said
"Friend of the bride or of the groom."

Because I knew them both quite well
I didn't know what to say,
He led me to a seat of his choice
As the minister began to pray.

A beautiful solo then followed,
The guy had a wonderful voice,
The bride looked beautiful to all who hoped
This time she'd made a better choice.

The reception which followed was wonderful,
They had plenty of their friends there,
And those who failed to show up at all
Were the ones who really didn't care.

Remember the choices you make in life
Every day that you make it through,
If you give to others the best that you have
That is what will come back to you.

Charles Lee Taylor

The Word

My dear friend have you not heard,
Although some may consider it odd,
That in the beginning was The Word,
It was alive and dwelt with God.

The power of the Almighty King
Was given to THE SON,
God really did not have to do that
For the three of them are one.

When Jesus came to spread the word
Nothing more important could He say
Than in our desire to reach our home on high
That He is the only way.

Man was created and loved by God,
It didn't happen the other way,
If we do not try to get things right
There'll be a debt we will not wish to pay.

We all will have an eternal life
Which we must begin someday,
Will you now accept what Jesus did
Or in the end will you have to pay?

Charles Lee Taylor

This Is The Way

Our Father,
Who sits on a throne,
Gave us Jesus,
So we would never be alone.

For whoever believeth in Him shall not perish
But have eternal life,
The Lord detests the way of the wicked,
But pursues those who do right.

The Lord, my God, is with me,
And He's mighty to save,
He was with you at birth,
And He'll be with you at your grave.

He'll rejoice over you with music,
And soothe you with a song,
He'll supply you with an angel
To remind you when you're wrong.

Then, no matter which way
Your life begins to sway,
An angel will tap on your shoulder
And say, "This is the way."

By Phil Cruz
And dedicated to Mr. Charles Lee Taylor
And family

Thru The Light

As I watched "TV" some days ago
A lady spoke of when she died,
She was so moved by what she said,
Along with us, she almost cried.

She got sick and had to be hospitalized
And slipped into a coma for days,
She was aware when time came to leave her body
And travel some uncharted ways.

Her heart had stopped, her pulse was gone,
Doctors could find no sign of life,
Her death would cause pain in several others
For she was a mother and a wife.

She saw, and approached, the brightest light
And when she had traveled there thru,
Finding friends and relatives who had died before
To bid her welcome and show her what to do.

But suddenly she felt a powerful pull
Which was strong and it came from the rear,
She soon found out that she would have
To leave that place to return here.

When Jesus wept at the tomb of His friend
Could it have been because He knew
To be where he was, was the best place of all,
Yet He did what He had to do.

Charles Lee Taylor

To Prince

You lived for, lo, some fifteen years
You were a real good boy,
And as I write looking through my tears
I remember the years of joy,

You gave to this family, all of us,
You were more than a pet and/or friend,
You lived your life never making a fuss
From the day we got you until the end.

We shall miss you now as we enter the house,
As you wagged from one end to the other,
You treated this family in such a way
We have lost a son and a brother.

This family shall miss you, yes one and all,
To lose you has been very hard,
But we know in our hearts when you left our house
That you, Arctic Prince, are now walking with God.

Charles Lee Taylor

To Share

Some people seem to have so much
While others have nothing at all,
The space between keeps growing
But their cries on deaf ears fall.

One person can only use so much,
But they become as blind as can be
When it concerns giving some aid
To the poor which he cannot see.

Holding on tightly to what you have
Can make you miss lots of fun,
Along with the pleasure which sharing gives
As you help others one by one.

If you think that you are one
Who has much more than you need,
Then help someone else who needs you
And that help turns into a seed.

Your life, as well as the one you helped,
From that day could be so much better,
Mother Nature wishes you a quality life
And she'll send it to you if you'll let her.

Charles Lee Taylor

Traveling On Your Knees

Last night I took a journey
To a land across the seas.
I didn't go by ship or plane
I travelled on my knees.

I saw so many people there
In bondage to their sin,
And Jesus told me I should go,
That there were souls to win.

But I said "Jesus, I can't go
To lands across the seas."
He answered quickly, "Yes, you can
By travelling on your knees."

He said, "You pray, I'll meet the need.
You can, and I will hear.
It's up to you to be concerned
For lost souls far and near."

And so I did; knelt in prayer,
Gave up some hours of ease,
And with the Savior by my side,
I travelled on my knees.

As I prayed on, I saw souls saved
And twisted persons healed,
I saw God's workers strength renewed
While laboring in the field.

I said, "Yes Lord, I'll take the job.
Your heart I want to please.
I'll heed Your call and swiftly go
By travelling on my knees.

Author Unknown

Treating Others

Around the corner I have a friend
In this great city, which has no end,
Yet the days go by and weeks rush on
And before I know it another year has gone.

I never see my old friends' face
For life is a swift and terrible race,
He knows I like him just as well
As in the days when I rang his bell.

He rang mine, but we were younger then,
And now we are busy, tired old men,
Tired of playing a foolish old game,
Tired of trying to make a name.

"Tomorrow", I say, "I'll call Jim
Just to let him know I'm thinking of him!"
But tomorrow comes and tomorrow goes
And the distance between us grows and grows.

Around the corner, yet miles away,
"Here's a telegram, Sir. Jim died today."
And that's what we get and deserve in the end,
Around the corner, a vanished friend.

Unknown

Trip Home

Did you ever take a trip back home
Just to let your mom and dad
Know just how much they are loved by you
Because of the childhood you had?

You know, as they, things were not always
As you desired them to be,
But making the best of what you had
Opened the door to opportunity.

As they and you together
Always, did the best you could
To maximize opportunities that came
By your house or in the 'hood.

Because what they did for you back then
Got you to where you are today,
But all things get even better
If they taught you how to pray.

There was no divine mistake at hand
When God gave you the parents He did,
They were His choice to help you grow
Into adulthood from a little kid.

To thank and honor your parents
Is to do the same to God,
If you now know the tougher role
Don't spoil the child by sparing the rod.

Charles Lee Taylor

Trip To Aruba

I FINALLY GOT THE CHANCE TO GO
TO ARUBA ONCE AGAIN,
WE HIT A BIG SNAG IN SAN JUAN
AND ALMOST COULDN'T GET ON THE PLANE.

WE WERE TRAVELING "NON-REV" THAT DAY,
MY WIFE, YOUNGEST DAUGHTER AND ME,
WHEN WE WERE CALLED TO BOARD THE
PLANE,
THERE WAS ROOM FOR ONLY TWO, NOT
THREE.

MY WIFE AND I CONTINUED THE TRIP,
OUR DAUGHTER WE LEFT BEHIND,
SHE RAN INTO ONE OF HER FRIENDS
WHO PROVED TO BE CONCERNED AND KIND.

SHE WAS TOLD SHE WOULD CONTINUE THE
TRIP,
EVEN THOUGH SHE WAS FILLED WITH
GLOOM,
BUT GOD STILL SMILED AS HE LOOKED HER
WAY
FOR THAT NIGHT SHE WAS GIVEN A ROOM.

THE NEXT DAY EVERYTHING LOOKED MUCH
BETTER,
ALL THINGS SEEMED TO FALL INTO PLACE,
HER MOTHER AND I WERE FILLED WITH JOY
WHICH INCREASED WHEN WE SAW HER FACE.

OUR STAY IN ARUBA WAS OUTSTANDING,
I CANNOT TELL A LIE,
TO ROAM THE BEACHES WAS A LOT OF FUN
AND MOST PLEASING TO THE EYE.

YOU GUYS HAVE VACATION TIME COMING,
I SUGGEST THIS IS WHAT YOU DO,
TAKE YOUR LADY LOVE TO ARUBA,
SHE AND IT WILL BRING JOY TO YOU.

By Charles Lee Taylor
5-2-03

Trust God

I'd fly away, was what I heard,
If I had wings like that beautiful bird,
Another voice said, Oh no, not I,
God never intended that man should fly.

Did He plan that it would take all day
To visit a friend who lives five miles away?
When our eyes are dim and our bodies old,
That we be hungry and our houses cold?

Most of the things that we go through
Are not because of God but because of me and you,
Whether you are in the sunlight or in the shade
Is a direct result of the choices that you made.

Be a man, stand up and admit what you do,
The Father is still able to take care of you,
He said He would never leave you alone,
We're in trouble when we step out on our own.

Charles Lee Taylor

Truth

Some folk say that GOD is all love
But, in that, I cannot agree,
If you study HIS word and learn the truth
It is that truth that will set you free.

There are seven things that GOD does hate
That are recorded in the book,
Whether the first is most important I can't say
But I know it is "A proud look."

Then comes "one who knows not the truth"
And "He who kills without reason."
Then "One who plans to do others harm"
And "Another who is off to do evil".

There are some other things within the list,
Take your bible off the shelf
And turn to "Proverbs 6:16
Then read all of them for yourself.

God's actions may always come from love,
His motives are hard, fast and sound,
But should you be one who does it your way
He knows how to turn you around.

Charles Lee Taylor

"Unless They Are Prayed"

A LIFE WITHOUT PURPOSE IS BARREN
INDEED,
THERE CAN'T BE A HARVEST UNLESS YOU
PLANT A SEED,
THERE CAN'T BE ATTAINMENT UNLESS
THERE'S A GOAL,
A MAN IS BUT A ROBOT UNLESS THERE'S A
SOUL.

IF WE SEND NO SHIPS OUT, NO SHIPS WILL
COME IN,
AND UNLESS THERE'S A CONTEST NO ONE
CAN WIN,
FOR GAMES CAN'T BE WON UNLESS THEY
ARE PLAYED,
PRAYERS CAN'T BE ANSWERED UNLESS THEY
ARE PRAYED.

WHATEVER IS WRONG WITH YOUR LIFE
TODAY
YOU'LL FIND A SOLUTION IF YOU WILL
KNEEL TO PRAY,
NOT JUST FOR PLEASURE, ENJOYMENT OR
HEALTH,
NOT JUST FOR HONORS, PRESTIGE OR
WEALTH.

BUT PRAY FOR A PURPOSE TO MAKE LIFE
WORTH LIVING,
AND PRAY FOR THE JOY OF UNSELFISH
GIVING,
FOR GREAT IS YOUR GLADNESS AND RICH IS
YOUR REWARD
WHEN YOU MAKE YOUE LIFE'S PURPOSE THE
CHOICE OF
THE LORD

Author Unknown

Watching You

This morning I watched as you opened your eyes
For the first time to greet this day,
I was drinking in all the beauty you showed
As you sent a big smile my way.

As you rolled over and opened your eyes
You look around as if you would see
Someone else there in the room with us
But there was no one in it but me.

I bent over and took you in my arms
And began to caress your face,
I felt that my love for you runs so deep
It must be a part of God's grace.

I know that you really love me,
You show it in everything that you do,
Please know within your heart of hearts
That I feel the same way about you.

I thank our God each day of my life
That He did not too long make me wait
Before He placed me with the one
He had chosen to be my soul mate.

Each day has been so much better
Because you are in my life,
God gave me the best when He gave you to be
My love, my best friend, my wife.

Charles Lee Taylor

We Celebrate

We celebrate Christmas every year
All around the earth,
The focus should be Jesus Christ
On this day of His birth.

He was THE FATHER'S gift to man,
Good tidings we still tell,
And should you accept Him have no fear,
For Heaven is your home, not Hell.

There is a point that should be made,
He is not a baby today,
The Father had given Him the task
To take all of our sins away.

He sought to please His Father
Before His time had come
To start the task that God had given Him,
Saving all of mankind, not just some.

They beat Him and nailed Him to a tree,
The sins of mankind He bore,
His Father was gone before He finished His work,
No, He is not a baby anymore.

By: Charles Lee Taylor

Wedding Day

Did you really mean the things you said
On that blessed day when you were wed?
To love your mate with a love so true
That it must come from the core deep within you.

To give to your mate all the things that you can
As you try to bring happiness to that woman or man,
Being with each other in sickness and in health,
Sharing all things, whether poverty or wealth.

Standing by your mate while forsaking all others
Which includes the parents, sisters or brothers,
Will the mate remain number one in your life
After children come bringing struggle and strife?

And how about the things it says love does not do,
Can you say here and now that applies to you?
Do you forgive and yet you remember
Something done in January when you reach December?

Did the "I" remain so strong in your life
Pushing aside others, children, husband or wife?
Then I say look back and see what you said
On that blessed day when you were wed.

Charles Lee Taylor

What I Wish

When I think back to when I was a child
There were many days I wished to run wild,
The adults around had to keep me in tow
Telling me where, when as well as how I should go.

I had a strong will to do things my way,
To pay no attention to what others would say,
Just wait a few years and I'll show you,
I'll be doing all the things that I wish to do.

As the years went by I checked my resources,
I found that I was still controlled by outside forces,
Things, which were once given, I now must buy
In order to provide for me, myself and I.

I still may not go where I may desire to go,
For society keeps our actions in tow,
There are still some things I would like to do,
But the system says "NO" to both me and you.

We now have youngsters of our own
Who tell us how they wish to be grown,
They say that we don't have a clue
As to what they, with regularity, do.

The beat goes on with each generation,
The rules all change throughout the nation,
To do things their way they might say "Beat it."
As they try so hard not to repeat it.

Charles Lee Taylor

What Would Jesus Do??

There are many things we must do in this life,
Be it for parent, child, husband or wife,
To get things right between me and you
Just ask the question, "What would Jesus do?"

When faced with doing one thing over another
Remember Him who sticks closer than a brother,
He will always help you to see thru
Anything as you ask, "What would Jesus do?"

If much has been given you, much is required,
By sharing your blessings others can be inspired,
No matter what you have it doesn't belong to you,
So keep asking the question, "What would Jesus do?"

He left His heavenly home, came to earth to show
His children on this tiresome road how life should go,
From its dawn until the day it is no longer new,
We all would do better if we ask, "What would Jesus do?"

Always treat others as you wish to be treated,
You may hear bad things but be sure not to repeat it,
Pay your debts to others as they should pay you,
These are the kind of things Jesus would do.

Charles Lee Taylor

Where Is God

In creating man many years ago
God gave us a free will,
Although many years have passed us by
We operate that way still.

God may stand at the door and knock
But we must let Him in,
Many continue to keep Him out,
We deny Him again and again.

When a really bad thing, a catastrophe,
Really comes and hits us hard,
A voice can be heard, maybe two or three,
Each of which wonders just where is God.

A shooting at school, a building destroyed,
Planes used as missiles in the air,
Panic is seen all over the place
And some of us said "God does not care."

Our founders wove God in the foundation
Of this great land of ours,
But today the opposite is the case
As we use our God given powers.

The shooting in school is understandable,
We don't allow God in there,
as we continue to deny access to Him
This does not show that He does not care.

God loves us today as He did back then
And desires to be a part of our life,
Put out a welcome mat and let Him in,
He can change child, husband or wife.

The way you may choose to use your free will
Is really up to you,
Remember that God is limited by what you say
As well as by what you do.

By: Charles Lee Taylor

Working For Him

There are many working in the vineyard
Winning souls for our loving God,
They worked so hard from sun to sun
To apply His word and to get things done.

If you wish to become the apple of His eye
Then get in His word, words to live by,
They point the way to just how we should live,
Like rather than to receive, it is better to give.

They also tell us that every knee shall bow,
There's nothing beyond "every" so bow to Him now,
His word teaches us to love and obey,
And to reach God in Heaven, Jesus is the only way.

Should you keep your bible on a shelf
I suggest you start to read it for yourself,
His word will become a real part of you
As you are shown what He wants you to do.

Charles Lee Taylor

You Decide

We should always be careful
Of what we both say and do,
For we can never be really sure
Of who's listening to or watching you.

Our conversation speaks volumes
Whether it be seen or heard,
We all can say without a doubt
That a picture speaks louder than a word.

We may wish to live on the edge
And do all the things we desire,
But should we cause another to fall
Our eternity may be spent in the fire.

The song is incorrect with the message
"Do what you want to do.",
There is a price to pay for what is done
And it is controlled by you.

We may believe that what we do
Is no one's business but our own,
I hope you will live so you will not stand
Before the bar of justice alone.

Charles Lee Taylor

Your Choice

The Lord is my shepherd
But He's not mine alone,
He belongs to everyone
Who claims Him as their own.

He stands at the door knocking,
Asking that you let Him in,
Once in He will sup with you
And deliver you from all sin.

This world is not our home
And at times the trip is hard,
If you choose wisely and keep the faith
You will spend eternity with God.

Heaven or Hell, the choice is yours,
It can be seen by what you do,
A merciful God on judgment day
Will hand you the ticket chosen by you.

It is better to believe than not to
And die and find that you are wrong,
If you were to reverse the two
That makes eternity very long.

By: Charles Lee Taylor

About The Author

CHARLES LEE TAYLOR WAS BORN THE SECOND SON OF JOHN HENRY TAYLOR AND LILLIA RINGGOLD TAYLOR IN 1932 IN GREENVILLE N.C. HE WAS EDUCATED IN THE PUBLIC SCHOOLS THERE AND UPON GRADUATION FROM C.M. EPPES HIGH SCHOOL IN JUNE OF 1950 ENROLLED AT N.C.'S A AND T UNIVERSITY THE FOLLOWING SEPTEMBER. AFTER 1 ½ YEARS THERE HE JOINED

THE USMC WHERE HE SERVED FOR THREE YEARS. IN 1955 HE MARRIED HIS LONGTIME LOVE, AMY L. SHIVERS. THEY SOON RELOCATED TO MARYLAND WHERE THEY STILL LIVE. THEY HAVE THREE CHILDREN, TWO GIRLS AND A BOY. WHEN THEY FIRST CAME TO MARYLAND CHARLES WORKED FOR THE PENNSYLVANIA RAIL ROAD AS A FREIGHT BRAKEMAN. BECAUSE OF THE DANGER, HIS WIFE ASKED HIM TO FIND ANOTHER JOB WHICH LED TO THE START OF HIS POSTAL CAREER. WHILE WORKING THERE HE DECIDED TO RETURN TO SCHOOL TO COMPLETE HIS UNDERGRADUATE WORK AND ENROLLED AS A STUDENT AT MORGAN STATE COLLEGE. A YEAR AFTER GETTING HIS DEGREE FROM THERE HE ENROLLED AS A GRADUATE STUDENT AT WESTERN MARYLAND COLLEGE WHERE HE EARNED HIS MASTER'S DEGREE IN ADMINISTRATION. BESIDES WORKING AT THE POST OFFICE DURING HIS CAREER, HE ALSO WORKED AT THE ENOCH PRATT LIBRARY, WOODSTOCK, AND THE BALTIMORE CITY PUBLIC SCHOOLS. HE RETIRED IN 1992.

THE POEMS IN THE BOOK ARE A COLLECTION WRITTEN OVER MANY YEARS. SOME OF THEM WERE WRITTEN BECAUSE OF WHAT HE WAS GOING THROUGH AT THE TIME, SOME BECAUSE OF A REQUEST OF A FRIEND, BUT ALL ARE FROM THE HEART. THERE IS A STORY ATTACHED TO EACH POEM, WHICH IS AS INTERESTING AS THE POEM ITSELF. SOME WERE WRITTEN TO SOMEONE, SOME FOR SOMEONE AND SOME ABOUT SOMEONE. EVEN NOW WHEN HE READS THEM HE IS TOUCHED AND THEY EVOKE DEEP EMOTIONS. HE HOPES THAT THEY WILL ALSO TOUCH THAT SPECIAL PLACE IN YOUR HEART.